VALERIE LOVE

How to Be a Christian Witch

Includes Initiation Instructions

Copyright © 2020 by Valerie Love

All rights reserved. No part of this publication may be reproduced, stored or transmitted in any form or by any means, electronic, mechanical, photocopying, recording, scanning, or otherwise without written permission from the publisher. It is illegal to copy this book, post it to a website, or distribute it by any other means without permission.

First edition

This book was professionally typeset on Reedsy. Find out more at reedsy.com

II DECLARE

What is a Declaration?	21
The Declaration	23
To Whom Are You Making the Declaration?	26
Initiation as a Christian Witch	28
Initiation Definition	28
The Trap	29
Initiation Considerations	32
Study of Magickal Systems	32
A Word About Timing	33
Initiation Grades	34
Grades of Initiation in the Covenant of Christian Witches Mystery School	35
Initiation Privacy & Safety Precautions	37
The Blood Oath	39
Proceed Safely	40
Procuring Blood for the Declaration	41
Your Birth Code	45
Galactic Signature	45
Numerology	46
Tarot Birth Cards	46
Western Astrology	47
Eastern Astrology	47
Birthday Psalm	48
The Initiator	52
Compensation for the Initiator	54
You Are Sovereign	55
Preparation for the Initiation	56
Initiatory Angel	57
Angelic & Planetary Days & Hours	58
Ruling Tarot Card	59
Ruling Bible Character	60

Contents

Introduction — vi
  Part 1 - Decide — vii
  Part 2 - Declare — vii
  Part 3 - Document — viii
  Part 4 - Do — viii
12 Divestments — x
What This Book Cannot Do For You — xiv
  A Word to Neophytes — xv
  Sovereignty — xv
  Trust — xviii
  Simply Sharing — xix

I DECIDE

The Ultimate Decision — 3
Decision #2 — 7
Decision #3 — 13
Decision #4 — 15
Decisions — 17

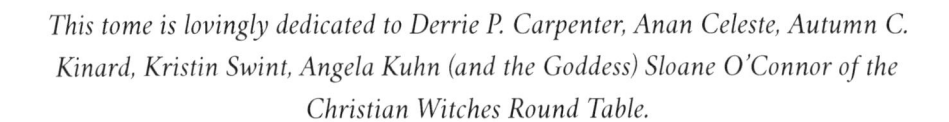

This tome is lovingly dedicated to Derrie P. Carpenter, Anan Celeste, Autumn C. Kinard, Kristin Swint, Angela Kuhn (and the Goddess) Sloane O'Connor of the Christian Witches Round Table.

Thank you for inviting me into your space, which felt like a soul hug from ancient, once lost and now found sisters.

Kudos to all of you for the powerful work you do to uplift and advance Christian Witches globally!

You are loved and appreciated.

Integrate the Elements	63
Select the Location	64
Select the Participants	65
Select the Initiatory Steps	65
Select Your Attire	65
Prepare the Reliquary	67
Fasting & Detox	68
The Banquet of Initiation	69
Prepare the Space	69
Consecration	70
Invocation of the Archangels	72
Construction of the Altar	73
Your New Sacred Name	75
Your Consecration	77
Consecration Steps	79
Prayer	80
Call in Your Spirit Team	80
Sacred Herbal Bath	81
Silence	83
Anointing Oil	83
White Attire	85
Crown Care	86
Initiatory Order of Rites	87
Sample Outline of the Initiatory Order of Rites:	88
Example of an Initiatory Order of Rites:	89
After the Initiation	102
Annual Ritual of Remembrance	103
How to Perform the Ritual of Remembrance	103

III DOCUMENT

Codify	107

IV DO

Magickal Implements	113
Bibles	114
Tarot Decks	115
Magick Wands	116
Crystals	117
The Magick Ring	117
Books, Books and More Books	118
Candles	118
Tools	119
Grimoires	119
Apothecary	120
Practicing Magick	122
The Laws of Magick	124
The Cosmos	125
The Process	126
Start Here	128
Invocation vs. Evocation	129
Angel Magick	129
Summoning Demons	130
Terrestrial Spirits	130
Do Something	131
Emotional Toxicity & Magick	132
Your Golem	133
What to Clear	134
How to Clear the Emotional Body	136
Desired States	138
29 Annual Rituals	141
12 New Moons	142
12 Full Moons	143
The Winter Solstice	143
The Spring Equinox	143

The Summer Solstice	143
The Fall Equinox	144
Coven Formation	145
Equanimity	146
Law	146
Size	146
Birth Date of the Coven	148
Coven Opening Ritual	148
Commitment	148
Coven Agreement	149
Meeting Frequency	150
Location	151
Online Covens	151
Coven Leadership	151
Coven Name/Bible Character	152
Coven Colors	153
The Reliquary	153
Coven Meeting Agenda	154
Coven Services	155
Coven Grimoire	155
3-Part Clarion Call to Christian Witches Everywhere	156
1 - EXIT THE BROOM CLOSET	156
2 - SPEAK UP	159
3 - SHARE YOUR GIFTS	159
About the Author	161
Also by Valerie Love	163

Introduction

It's one thing to declare oneself a Christian Witch. It's a whole other matter entirely to put legs on this declaration and actually BE a Christian Witch.

Welcome to the path that is love of Christ and the Craft. There are millions of soulful ways to express and practice love of Christ and the Craft.

THERE IS NO ONE WAY TO DO IT.

Additionally: **THERE IS NO RIGHT WAY TO DO IT.** Therefore, what must follow is: **THERE IS NO WRONG WAY TO DO IT.**

Now that we've gotten those out of the way, let's proceed to the most important matter at hand: *how YOU are going to do it*.

I think this may be the ultimate reason you picked up this book: to determine how YOU will be a Christian Witch.

Though we can gain inspiration from others, the path of the Christian Witch is deeply personal and extremely unique to each Witch.

While there is no set-in-stone formula, there are THEMES, GUIDELINES and IDEAS that circulate among Christian Witches. That's what this book will explore: the themes that surface frequently when it comes to being a Christian Witch. We'll also cover initiation, rituals and practices for Christian Witches (which you can adopt, ignore or modify for your soul's fulfillment). You'll also find here experiences I've had as a Christian Witch as well as resources for Christian Witches all along the way. You'll also find a plentitude of books and websites I use in my magickal practice and am heartily recommending to you. I do not recommend what I don't use myself, and do not recommend what I have not found to be highly valuable. With that said, if you're reading the eBook version of this work, many of the links you'll find here are affiliate links, which means we earn a small commission if you choose to make a purchase using the link.

What you won't necessarily find here are the beliefs held by Christian Witches. I don't believe a blanket belief system exists for Christian Witches. I've written the book titled **Christian Witches Manifesto**, which outlines the 10 tenets which I myself hold dear as a Christian Witch, if that proves helpful to you in creating your own Christian Witches Manifesto.

This book is organized into 4 categories:

Part 1 - Decide

This is bar none the most important of all. Nothing happens until we ***decide***. The word decide, with the prefix 'de' (meaning 2 or dual) and 'cide' (kill) literally means to kill duality. Take the ONE road for Self. You know this road. It's your unique road. You can't NOT know this road. It's been speaking to you, calling you, whispering your name and beckoning you for the entire time you've been in a physical body. You can choose to answer the call of your soul, or not. There's no compulsion in spirituality. You get to DECIDE. And if at any juncture you don't like what you've chosen (or its outcomes), you get to CHOOSE AGAIN. This is at the core of your limitless, divine power.

Part 2 - Declare

A declaration is defined as " a formal or explicit statement or announcement" or "the formal announcement of the beginning of a state or condition." Who are you making this declaration to? **SELF.** The most important person in your world is **YOU**. Not mama, not daddy, not pastor, not teacher, not the butcher, baker or candle stick maker. **YOU are the most important and most powerful entity in YOUR LIFE.** What you say is gospel in your life. What are you declaring? The decision, intention and commitment to be a Christian Witch. The declaration is sealed with rituals of consecration and initiation should you so choose.

Part 3 - Document

Document your journey. Document means "a piece of written, printed, or electronic matter that provides information or evidence or that serves as an official record." The most important experiences in life carry with them heavy documentation. Signatures. Pictures. Agreements. Contracts. Why? Because the most important events in our lives deserve to be remembered, regarded as turning points, and preserved. Your Initiation Declaration and grimoire can serve as documentation as well as any other evidence that becomes a part of the official record of you being a Christian Witch.

Part 4 - Do

This section of the book is all about taking ACTION… to move in the direction or the calling. To me, being a Christian Witch is a calling. (I talk more about this in my book **Christian Witches Manifesto**.) Taking action is the juiciest part! DOING what we came here to DO. Being who we came here to BE. WALKING our talk! I'm so happy we're on this journey together. Please know you're surrounded by thousands of Christian Witches all over the GLOBE, each practicing in their own magnificent way, loving this path.

Before we dive in, keep the #1 charge in spirituality at the forefront of your consciousness: **KNOW THYSELF**. To know oneself is to know the universe.

Next, I'm offering a prayer for us. It's a prayer I wrote many years ago when it struck me in the gut just how invested I was in what other people thought of me. DIVESTING oneself of the need for approval or acceptance or validation is critical on this path, perhaps more critical than other paths. Paths that are deemed 'acceptable' by the mass consciousness don't draw the ire of other people. Quite the contrary. When we join a church on Sunday morning at the altar call, everyone in the church cheers and is overjoyed that we 'came to Jesus.'

It's unlikely you'll meet with cheers from those who are not Christian Witches (or who are not friends of Christian Witches, of which there are many). It's more likely that you'll meet with people who do not yet understand that one can love Christ and the Craft.

It matters not what people understand, nor what they say.

What matters in your life is YOU.

Let's begin.

12 Divestments

Christian Witches Prayer of RELEASE from What Others Think

God/Goddess/I AM
Great Spirit, Wakan Tanka, Creator of All,

I confess I have been fearful...
I've overly concerned myself with people... what people say... and what effects I think people could have on me.

In those moments, I have forgotten my Essential Divine Nature as a Child of the Heavens.
I allowed my mind to be consumed with fearful thoughts, causing a dangerous downward spiral. My emotions quickly followed... tumbling into the darkness... ripping at my soul.

NO MORE.

I NOW make and commit to the following 12 DIVESTMENTS:

DIVESTMENT #1:
I DIVEST MYSELF of all fret, worry, concern and/or fear about what other people think. What other people think is their business. What I think is my business.

I ALONE RULE MY MIND.

DIVESTMENT #2:
I DIVEST MYSELF of thinking I know what other people think. I cannot know what others think. I know what I think. MY MIND IS MY OWN POWERFUL DOMAIN.

DIVESTMENT #3:
I DIVEST MYSELF of thinking I should know what other people think. I shouldn't know anything other than what I know. I CHOOSE to KNOW THYSELF.

DIVESTMENT #4:
I DIVEST MYSELF of all fret, worry, concern and/or fear over being accepted, liked, approved of, validated, and/or ANY other co-dependent, dysfunctional reliance on ANY approval from the outside.
Inside my soul, Source approves of me, which means I APPROVE OF ME.

DIVESTMENT #5:
I DIVEST MYSELF of attempting to moderate and/or edit my True Self to 'fit in' and/or not rock the proverbial boat. Though I do not create conflict, I am not afraid to end it. I AM a change-maker. The world will never be the same, all because God Herself chose to show up to this planet as me.

DIVESTMENT #6:
I DIVEST MYSELF of shrinking ANY aspect of myself to fit the construct of normalcy as created, dictated and perpetuated by mass fear consciousness. I AM here to emanate and reverberate Love. LOVE EXPANDS. I AM ONLY HERE FOR LOVE.

DIVESTMENT #7:
I DIVEST MYSELF of doing it all myself, doing it by myself, or doing it only for myself. I AM on a Divine Plan. I AM divinely guided from the heart well

within, my inner cauldron. I walk in the Presence. I AM a Perfect, Illumined Thought in the Mind of God/Goddess/I AM.

DIVESTMENT #8:
I DIVEST MYSELF of wishing I had not been born a Witch. I know God/Goddess/I AM created me in this magickally delicious way for a magickally delicious purpose. I TRUST and KNOW I AM and HAVE ALL I require for my PERFECTLY SCRUMPTIOUS LIFE DIVINE AS A WITCH!

DIVESTMENT #9:
I DIVEST MYSELF of ALL fear, worry, panic, concern, edginess, nervousness, doubt, teeth-chattering, nail-biting, knee-knocking thoughts, feelings, words and actions. My attitudes, actions, habits and behaviors are beautifully orchestrated by CHRIST. I AM A LIVING, BREATHING, MOVING SYMPHONY OF THE LIFE DIVINE, THE MAGNIFICENT CHRIST CONSCIOUSNESS THAT CONQUERS ALL.

DIVESTMENT #10:
I DIVEST MYSELF of thinking I know what's best for me. The tiny human frail and fearful mind has no idea of what's best for me, or what would make me ultimately happy, and will only lead me in pathways of pain at every possible turn. I TRUST in and MOVE in the Guidance of Source. I CHOOSE the path of JOY.

DIVESTMENT #11:
I DIVEST MYSELF of ALL unworthiness, undeservedness and resistance to RECEIVING the DELICIOUSLY LUSCIOUS life experience on planet earth my soul signed up for before my physical body showed up here. SINCE IT IS MY FATHER'S GOOD PLEASURE TO GIVE ME THE KINGDOM, IT IS MY GOOD PLEASURE TO ACCEPT IT.

DIVESTMENT #12:
I DIVEST MYSELF of ALL guilt, shame, judgment and all their bastard

children. I CHOOSE TO REMEMBER I AM HOLY, INNOCENT, PURE, and CLEAN. I AM FORGIVEN of EVERYTHING. I AM THE WHOLLY HOLY CHILD OF A WHOLLY HOLY CREATOR.

Having made these 12 DIVESTMENTS, and committing to the same... BY MY FIERCE COMMAND, this FIAT now takes on FORM AND FLESH, making itself apparent in EVERY area of my life experience in ways that totally and completely bliss me out, delight my spirit, sing my heart and dance my soul.

I AM THANKFUL, GREAT SPIRIT, CREATRIX of ALL, for the LOVE of this Great Uni-Verse of Splendor that responds to my every prayer, IMMEDIATELY relaying the very BEST answer to me in PURE BLISS and BEAUTY.

I AM THAT I AM
So Mote It Be
Ase

What This Book Cannot Do For You

Over the years, we've received multitudinous questions (which could easily number into the thousands) and requests for help from new Christian Witches, such as:

- What kind of wand should I use?
- What holidays do I celebrate?
- What are our rituals?
- Where do I start?
- What do I do on the full moon/new moon?
- What kind of spells should I be doing?
- I'm a Christian Witch, help!

For several years, I've been quietly observing questions such as these, and many others, on our **Christian Witches Facebook Fan Page**, and in Christian Witches Facebook Groups, in emails, personal messages on social media and messages received at the **Christian Witches website**. With an intention to be supportive to those who are earnestly seeking, I'll offer first a word to neophytes, then a little tough love in the form of 2 distinct issues to be addressed here: **SOVEREIGNTY** and **TRUST**.

A Word to Neophytes

A neophyte is defined as: "a person who is new to a subject, skill, or belief" or "a novice in a religious order." There's a broad range in being a neophyte to Christian Witchcraft, from just discovering it yesterday all the way to knowing about it for many years, yet only now beginning to intentionally practice. Only you know if you're a neophyte.

If you are a neophyte, **CONGRATULATIONS** on stepping into this magnificent soul calling! I applaud you. And, I encourage you with these words from the Holy Bible penned by Paul in a letter to a young man he was mentoring, Timothy:

"Study to shew thyself approved unto God, a workman that needeth not to be ashamed, rightly dividing the word of truth." - 2 Timothy 2:15 (KJV)

The operative words here are 'study' and 'workman.' Study is crucial, yet beyond study, we must **WORK**. That's what this book will invite you to do: engage **YOUR WORK** of becoming a masterful and powerful Christian Witch.

Sovereignty

You are the ultimate authority in your life and world. Not you, the personality. YOU the divine. YOU that is one with Source. You are a **SOVEREIGN** being. The word sovereign is defined as "possessing supreme or ultimate power."

Ye are gods.

This means you are the supreme and ultimate power in your world. This is the most important mandate to remember as a Christian Witch. If you took this to heart, and threw out everything else in this book, I would not be offended.

It's my belief (I could be wrong, and I'm willing to be) that most people who ask a lot of questions of other people are lazy and irresponsible.

It's great to ask questions. It's how we learn and grow. For many of us, unanswered questions became the catalyst for striking out on our own to secure answers. I'm the creator of a Mystery School, with lots of students who asks lots of questions. Questions are encouraged on the spiritual path. Ask all the questions you desire.

The ultimate question is: who are you asking?

Source.

Turn your questions inward to Source.

This is not to say that you will never ask a question of another person. That would prove both ridiculous and impossible. We're in relationships with many people. We're all asking each other questions all the time.

I'm referring here to posing 'inward' questions to 'outer' people.

A boatload of the questions I see floating around are 'inward' questions. I'm not purporting that we (practicing and/or experienced Christian Witches) can't help you with this. We can. We can offer guidance, ideas, and our own experiences.

However, in order to stand in your spiritual maturity, agency and sovereignty, you must have a RESOLUTE, UNWAVERING WILLINGNESS and VOLUNTARY COMPULSION to do the DEEP INNER SPIRITUAL WORK that causes you to RADICALLY and RUTHLESSLY engage in PRAYER, MEDITATION and SPIRITUAL PRACTICES over MANY DECADES to DEVELOP, CULTIVATE and NURTURE a VISCERAL and TOTAL CONNECTION WITH SOURCE that becomes your TRUSTED INNER GUIDANCE that's ABSOLUTELY HEEDED from an inner rock solid foundation of FAITH and TRUST in every situation, above everything and everyone on the outside.

Whew. That's a mouthful.

In short, there's no shorting the process of doing your ***spiritual work***. That's where all your unique, beautifully individualized-for-you answers are to be sourced.

Many people don't want to do the work. They want others to do it for them. They want others to go fishing for them, clean the fish, season the fish, cook the fish and lay the whole meal before them.

Lazy. And irresponsible.

There is a better way.

We are all to go fishing for ourselves. We are all here to enthusiastically search for and find our own answers within. Christ promised that if we keep asking, we will be answered. If we keep knocking, the door will be opened. He was speaking metaphorically of the spiritual seeker.

Yes, you can seek out mentors, coven mates, accountability partners, coaches, guides and community. That search would be applauded and encouraged by this witch. I have lots of spiritual community around me. It's the self-loving thing to do on the spiritual path, as none of us could do this alone.

While a wise person will listen to the counsel of wise people, that one knows that the final decision is one's own. You alone have the ultimate power and authority to make the final and perfect call for you, at all times, without exception.

YOU ARE SOVEREIGN.

You're that powerful. The REAL YOU knows every answer. Tap this inner knowing. The REAL YOU knows EXACTLY how you're going to be a Christian Witch, and is indeed what brought you to this path in the first place.

How does one tap this INNER KNOWING?

MEDITATION. SILENCE. STILLNESS. PRAYER. SPIRITUAL PRACTICE.

Daily spiritual practice along with moment-by-moment availability to Spirit in order to transform self — and the world in the process — is a game-changer.

Keep doing that for decades. Then you're getting somewhere.

What's it all for? Well, that's another million dollar question.

We're becoming God. The crust of the not-self gives way to the splendor and beauty of the True Self. This is the Great Work. Individuation. Alchemy of the Soul. Ascension. Christ-hood. Buddha nature.

Yes, you're **becoming God**.

For me, whatever I have to do to become God is totally worth it.

— My calling as a Christian Witch

Trust

Now for the next issue: **TRUST**.

Many new Christian Witches may be looking for exact spells, formulas and how-to's.

I can understand this desire. It's safe. We feel safe if someone tells us what to do, how to do it, when to do it, who to do it with, and what the predictable outcome will be.

Though I can understand this request, it's not for the Christian Witch, or any seeker on the spiritual path for that matter. This is not to say that instructions or guidance aren't helpful. They are. This book is full of ideas you may find inspiring.

However, there's more. Spirituality is about self-agency and trusting yourself, among a myriad of other ingredients. It's about **EXPERIENTIAL LEARNING**, which means you get to enter the laboratory and make shit up, and sometimes blow shit up.

Experience is the best way to learn. Life is about having experiences. Experiences lead to wisdom. Wisdom leads to compassion.

If you attend a sweat lodge with those who use this as a spiritual practice, you'll gain far more from the experience than you ever could have from reading books about sweat lodges, asking other people about sweat lodges, watching sweat lodge videos on YouTube, and joining 50 million sweat lodge groups on Facebook.

I'd rather forgo the research and head directly into the sweat lodge if that's where Higher Self is leading me.

The spiritual path is full of **EXPERIENCES**. Experiences that ONLY you can have. Don't be afraid to engage this plethora of experiences. You've got to get out there and DO. You've got to self-initiate, go with your intuition and take radical action that seems illogical. Then you get to review the results, course correct and go for it again. This is the thrill ride of life!

It's my intuition that people who don't allow themselves to have this very experiential approach to life just don't trust themselves.

You cannot triumph on the spiritual path if you don't trust yourself. Trust that you got this. Trust that you know the Knower, thus the REAL YOU knows all the answers (without ever picking up a book or joining a Facebook group). Trust the universe. Trust timing. Trust the process.

I guess I'm asking you to simply **TRUST LIFE**... to be Key #0 in the Tarot: the Fool on the magnificent hero's quest, who leaps off the edge of the cliff with no worries, and doesn't even have sense enough to look down first.

Now that's how to really live! No, I'm not asking you to take ridiculous risks for no good reason, or to be foolish. I am asking you to TRUST and walk by FAITH and not by sight.

Simply Sharing

Now let's move to the next point: this book is me sharing with you. That's all. It's not a holy book. It's not a be-all-end-all. It's not a bible of Christian Witchcraft. This is simply one Christian Witch, sharing her experiences. I don't have anything else to give you.

The intention in sharing my experiences is simple: INSPIRATION. I pray this work will inspire you to greater heights of doing and being the REAL YOU: **GOD.**

To be clear: I'm not looking for zealots. I left a bunch of zealots when I chose to exit the cult of Jehovah's Witnesses. I'm not seeking disciples. Witches are not disciple material. I'm not looking for a new Christian Witches religion, or to start one. This is simply me sharing myself and my spiritual path with you.

Here's what this book cannot and will not do for you:

- It cannot tell you what you're supposed to be doing. Only you know that.
- It cannot make you right and other people wrong.
- It cannot make up for your unwillingness to do the very challenging, years-long spiritual work of delving deep within to develop and cultivate a visceral, palpable relationship with Source that will give you the answers you require in any and every given situation.

- It cannot make you spiritually mature. Only you, a decision and time can accomplish that.
- It cannot make up for a toxic emotional body (which will cause more harm than good if you attempt to practice magick, more on this later).
- It will not give you steps in a linear fashion that you must follow.
- It will not give you the exact words to say so you can escape the creative process of conjuring your own from the core of your soul, then trusting yourself enough to know that what you self-initiated will work better for you than anything anyone else could possibly give you.
- It will not give you everything there is to know about being a Christian Witch (that would require volumes). This book will give you a **FRAMEWORK** and a **STARTING POINT**. **PRACTICE** and **EXPERIENCE** will take your magick as a Christian Witch to the stratosphere.
- It will not give you anything you're ordained to seek and find within.

Remember: your Inner Knowing is your Ultimate Authority. You are SOVEREIGN. Period. End of story. The fat lady has sung.

I

DECIDE

Here we discuss the ultimate decision, along with 3 primary decisions you may be faced with as a Christian Witch. Let's dive in...

The Ultimate Decision

For me, as a Christian Witch, there was an ultimate decision to be made.

I felt the irresistible pull to the occult, even while in the Kingdom Hall (I was raised in the cult of Jehovah's Witnesses... you can read that real and raw story in my book ***Confessions of a Christian Witch***), and after leaving the cult, in church.

I joined a non-denominational church for awhile, looking for an alternative to the fundamentalist upbringing that had shackled my mind.

At the time, I didn't know what I was looking for; I only knew I was searching for **something**.

Dissatisfaction set me on the quest. No one who's deeply satiated goes looking for anything. Not only was I not satiated, I was starved. Soul-starved.

I devoured books on Buddhism, astrology, numerology, Wicca, the occult, magick, angels, demons, spirit communication, spells, spirit guides, animal totems, prayer, meditation and spirituality. I cannot tell you how many books I read when my hungry bear self first exited the cave.

Wicca was the closest thing to answering some of my questions, yet it didn't hit the nail on the head for me. While I had nothing against Wicca, it wasn't singing to my soul.

There had to be more.

Then it finally hit me! Like all truth, it had been there all along. Yes, I had Tarot decks, and I had Bibles. Yes, I had crystals and I had crosses. Yes, I had magick and I had miracles. **Nothing said I had to get rid of either.** I already had everything that fulfilled me spiritually, I just didn't consciously understand how to integrate it all. Wonder of wonders! The puzzle pieces were there all along, I just had to put this jigsaw together!

INTEGRATION.

For me, the most important decision I had to make — following my revelation that there was nothing to throw out, only an integration to experience — was to decide that I was going to move forward with being a Christian Witch, which would mean pulling together all the seemingly disparate aspects of my spiritual path thus far.

I didn't call myself a Christian Witch at the time. I had never heard the term before it flew out of my mouth in a burst of inspiration on a **YouTube video** I uploaded on October 22, 2011. That video went viral, for obvious reasons, and out came the haters.

Let's consider context. It's 2011. There are no Christian Witches Facebook Pages, Groups, YouTube Channels, Instagram accounts or websites. There was 1 resource in existence at the time: *The Path of a Christian Witch* by Adelina St. Claire. I didn't know about the book back then. Later, when I did learn of it, I was convinced that this was an amazing witch far ahead of her time. I applaud and salute her. (I haven't read the book, though I've heard it's a valuable resource.)

With that said, I had never heard the term 'Christian Witch' so when I heard myself say it, I was shocked. No forethought went into that video. Only inspiration.

Let's back up a tad.

When I arose that morning and engaged my spiritual practices, I heard inspiration from Source. I call it the Voice. It simply dropped 3 tiny words into my consciousness: 'tell your story.'

Well, as you can see, those 3 tiny words changed everything.

When I heard the words 'tell your story,' to me it meant: *'share what's happening for you on the spiritual journey Val.'* Easy enough, especially considering my YouTube channel is focused on spirituality.

The Ultimate Decision

The strange part was when the words "Christian Witch" fell out of my mouth.

This is just like Spirit. It was a simple, 2-word encapsulation of what had likely taken decades on the spiritual path, lifetimes even, to realize.

After recording the video in which I heard myself say something as inflammatory as "Christian Witch," I had a sense of what was about to happen. Fear slithered through my body like a serpent — belly turning, heart racing fear — nearly aborting the upload.

Thankfully, something in me (let's call it the soul) was bigger than the tiny, frail, afraid, human me. The big Self lit a bonfire in the cauldron of my heart, compelling me to upload the video in the face of what could have been paralyzing fear.

That day changed everything.

Before the video, I had one understanding of my path.

After the video, not only was I completely clear that I was integrating what appeared to be 2 distinct (and even diametrically opposed) belief systems: Christ on one hand, and the Craft on the other, I also now had a name for it.

Could these two live together? Peacefully? Productively? Purposefully?

I had no idea… yet I was willing to find out.

I made the all important *decision* to go in that direction. A decision that didn't require a committee of other people. I am a committee of one. You are a committee of one.

I made the decision to go with the intuitive knowing that I am indeed a Christian Witch, and indeed had been one all along, even before I had languaging for it.

Make the decision.

Next steps are never shown to us until we *decide*. You **DECIDE**. The universe **ANSWERS**.

Make the decision today that you are walking the way of the Christian Witch with your head held high, no matter what, blissfully integrating your Christ consciousness with all your witchy deliciousness.

Now that you've made that first decision, let's move forward together to examine a few more radical decisions we're faced with on this intriguing journey of being a fully integrated Christian Witch.

Decision #2

After having made the ultimate decision that I was indeed forging ahead into completely unknown territory as a Christian Witch, it quickly became apparent that many more decisions would have to be made along the way.

One of the next big decisions was the choice of whether I would keep this very important soul matter to myself, or share it with the people around me.

By this time, I had long left the cult of Jehovah's Witnesses. I was altogether unwilling to live by their rules. They knew I was into all kinds of supernatural things, and I was perfectly okay with that. I had been disfellowshipped from the organization (ex-communicated), so the Witnesses couldn't speak to me, and hence were no longer a big part of my life.

At this juncture, I had ensconced myself in the metaphysical community in the DMV (DC, Maryland and Virginia). At our functions, we often wore all white.

Other than my metaphysical, witchy, Tarot-reading friends in spiritual community, people around me at the time consisted of ex-JW friends who chose to stay in touch, neighbors, a few family members who were no longer deep in the cult and thus could still communicate with me, work mates, and my Baptist husband and his family.

I will say that it's likely everyone in my orbit knew I was not strictly Christian. Yes, I went to church, almost every Sunday. I went on a missions trip to Kenya with a church group of 18 people. I wore white much of the time. I had my crown wrapped. One of the evangelists in the missions group kept looking at me sideways. When she tried to make me fall out by hitting me, and it proved unsuccessful, she whispered in my ear "you better give up all that Buddha shit." Wow. Thank you evangelist. If you hit me one more time (she was making her second round to hit people again who didn't fall out the first time), I'm from the hood and there will be a problem.

Though they couldn't quite figure out what was going on, the Christians around me had their suspicions.

Do I tell anyone? Do I tell tell everyone?

Years before making the very public declaration on YouTube, I was met with the decision of who I would be willing to tell in my personal life. Though I didn't have the language for being a Christian Witch before the YouTube video, I was witchy, and I was Christian.

Did I have to come out and tell them the whole, raw, real, microscopic truth?

This is a decision fraught with danger from the start.

Why? Because we can never be too careful when attempting to accurately ascertain our deepest motivations and drivers.

If my decision was not to tell anyone, I would had to honestly ask myself: is this the shadow running the show? With its collection of haunting memories from multiple painful outcasts I had experienced as a child or in past lives? If that's the case, fear is definitely running the show.

Or, was it that I was choosing to be private (not secretive, not hiding) which could be completely self-nurturing?

Time for a heaping dose of radical self honesty.

I had had a long history of people pleasing, trying to fit in, needing external validation and a whole host of other fear-based issues that kept me from sharing the truth about myself in any given situation (and not just around being a Christian Witch).

I had lived a good portion of my life being afraid of the judgment of other people. What I did not know then — which is abundantly clear now — is that I could not have possibly experienced the judgment of anyone else unless I was unconsciously judging myself.

Inner critic be damned.

So, what decision would I make?

I decided to go the vulnerable route, and let myself be seen for who I truly am by the people I most loved and who most loved me. I chose to give myself the opportunity to be loved for who I truly am, witch and all. After all, unconditional love means acceptance and non-judgment, right?

I started with my Baptist husband. Here's the story.

We were to take a weekend trip to his family's home, about a 3-hour drive from where we lived, for our usual Mother's Day visit. There was a conflict: the 1-day Tarot workshop I had secretly registered for fell on the same weekend. It would be highly abnormal for me not to join my hubby and the kids for Mother's Day at his mom's. I couldn't just not go.

I thought it through. I decided to attend the Tarot workshop on Saturday, then take the drive in my own car to mom's afterward. Though I would arrive late Saturday night, probably a bit worn out, I would still be present for the Mother's Day festivities with the family on Sunday.

It seemed like the perfect plan.

I communicated to hubby that I had an important workshop on Saturday (not unusual for me). I shared the plan with him: he and the kids could go to his mom's on Friday night as usual. I would join them on Saturday night after my workshop.

Thankfully, he didn't ask many questions. I guess I was convincing enough.

As I write this to you in the year 2020, I reflect on the Valerie of 15 years ago and send her copious amounts of heaping, steamy love. She was so brave, even though she didn't know what the hell she was doing.

I promise you I was making it all up as I went along.

Back to the story.

I saw the hubby and kids off on Friday night and sank into a beautiful evening prepping for my first ever Tarot workshop the next day. I eyed the closet deciding I would go with something sparkly. *Yes, Tarot deserves sparkly attire.*

I don't know why I was so nervous. It could have been because forbidden actions are the most delectable.

The next morning I had an amazing breakfast and was off to the spiritual center just outside of Washington, D.C. to meet my first Tarot teacher ever, Geraldine Amaral.

I wasn't ready.

I was, however, **willing**. Remember, the spiritual path requires you to act before you're ready.

The Tarot workshop blew my mind and left me ravenous for more. The entire class went deep that day, reading each other under our instructor's loving guidance. My Tarot teacher watched me read Tarot for the first time and remarked "you're a natural!" I felt proud of my choices. This was all so… **right**.

The whole affair constituted a major upheaval in consciousness. I would never be the same. *How was I supposed to show up to the family tonight acting 'normal?'*

There was no way.

After it was all said and done, I hopped in my car for the 3-hour drive. It was over before I realized it. For the entire drive, Tarot swirled through my consciousness. It was as if the characters in the deck whom I had just been reunited with from a past life (or many past lives) danced their celebratory hypnotic rhythm in a swirl about my head, akin to a halo.

Welcome home witch.

I'm sure I was glowing when I arrived at my mother-in-law's. And still wearing the sparkly outfit. The sparkly outfit wasn't strange for me.

Would everyone be able to see how sparkly my aura was? Oh this is not going to end well for me! I'm headed through the door of my Baptist family! What was I thinking?!?

The best thing to do is CONFESS Valerie.

I'll pause the story here for a moment. Don't ask me why the act of sharing my spiritual path with people I love was viewed then as tantamount to a confession. That's just where I was with it all. I felt as if I'd been sneaking around behind my partner's back. Cheating.

You can't cheat with Tarot, Valerie. Yet that's how I felt.

Decision #2

I walked in the door sparkly. All the gathered family members greeted me with exhilaration as per usual. No one sniffed Tarot on me yet. But then again, would they? They're church folk. *Would church folk even know what Tarot smells like?*

I couldn't be sure. I moved with stealth.

Of course, the question would come up as to why I didn't come with my husband and kids on Friday like normal. My whole little normal life seemed to be going to shreds, and fast. How could one meet the Emperor, or the Wheel of Fortune, or the Queen of Pentacles and still be normal?

Good thing my husband had already announced to the family that I'd be attending a business workshop that day and would be arriving late.

Did I say I was going to a business workshop? Did I unintentionally convey to him that I was doing some kind of business activity?

Oh Lord. This is getting worser and worser! Ok. That's it. I gotta come clean. This is killing me!

Later that night, after everyone had gone to bed, save me, my husband and his sister, he and I had a powerful conversation behind closed doors in the guest bedroom we always slept in when visiting his mom.

The conversation would literally alter the flavor and trajectory of our entire relationship.

I told him. I came out and said I had gone to a Tarot workshop that day and that I found it to be exquisite. I went on about how amazing it was and that the Tarot teacher told me I was a natural. I felt like I had been reading Tarot all my life, I shared honestly.

His mouth hung open. Flabbergasted is a good word to describe his shock.

Somehow, he had convinced himself — or assumed — that I was at a business meeting. Maybe that was my unconscious doing. And now, to hear that I was away from the family at a Tarot workshop was too unbelievable for him to even bear.

He walked out the guest bedroom after the conversation.

I didn't know where he was going.

Turns out, he had gone upstairs to where his sister was (whom he's quite close to) to tell her the story of where his wife really was that day.

Betrayal. Lies. Deceit. Hiding. Secrecy. And the abomination of Tarot, the devil's picture book.

That's what seemed to waft through the air. When I found him and his sister talking about it upstairs (something led me to go seek him out to be sure he was okay), I was mortified. I didn't anticipate that he would go and tell my secret so promptly.

Right then and there, in the middle of the upstairs movie room in my mother-in-law's home, it became public knowledge that I was now a Tarot reader.

Decision #3

Somewhere along this delicious, unfolding journey of being a Christian Witch, I was faced with yet another decision: am I going to stay in church?

By the time I came to this choice point, I was far removed from the fundamentalist upbringing of my youth. I was in favor of — and a member of — a non-denominational mega-church in the neighborhood.

I loved it. It seemed to be quite a bit looser than the brand of religion I was accustomed to in fundamentalist Christianity. I also loved that it didn't have the hierarchy of the Baptist Church or the A.M.E. Church my husband frequented, and that I would often attend.

I do love a good choir. And the high vibration. And the feeling I have in praise and worship. There's nothing like it.

Yet I was also becoming more sensitive to the fact that most Christian churches, A.M.E., Baptist or non-denominational, seemed to have favorite people that they loved to hate. Gay people. Lesbian people. Transgender people. And witches.

There was a special disdain reserved for these groups. The way they would speak in church when referring to any of these groups felt to me like the ultimate slap in the face.

I came to the conclusion that my soul was not going to fully thrive in church.

That was my decision.

That's not every Christian Witch's decision.

There are lots of Christian Witches and Catholic Witches who love attending and participating in church. I still love church as well, for visits.

For me, there's a distinction between visiting church — when invited or inspired — and being a card-carrying member.

I realized that my occult mind had drawn me far beyond the church. There was no going back. I couldn't be a member anymore, showing up every Sunday with a 'praise the Lord saints' and being a volunteer in the next drive/ministry/outreach.

Church membership no longer fed my soul like the magickal practices I had begun delving deeper into. I loved magick, craved it even, couldn't get enough. The more I devoured, the more the universe would send my way. I was in heaven.

Conversely, if I showed up in church and heard a witch slur, or faulty belief systems about witches working in tandem with the devil, it wouldn't align with me on the inside and what I knew to be the truth.

I made the decision to love church, yet not be a member of any given church.

I learned that I am the church. Nature is a church. The whole world is a church.

This is a decision only you can make. Whatever decision you make in support of your soul is for you and you alone. Let no one, not Witch or Christian, shame you or disrespect you for your choice.

This is your decision alone. If you choose wisely from deep within the cauldron of your heart, it will be the right choice for you.

Decision #4

Yet another decision floated up before me: am I going to join/form a coven or am I going to be a solitary, practicing Christian Witch?

Though I haven't joined a coven yet (or formed one), I'm a proponent of the idea, especially for Christian Witches. For us, a coven may be more important than it is for other traditions of Witchcraft. Why? Because almost every witchy and/or magickal path — from Hoodoo to Vodun to Gardnerian Wicca to Alexandrian Wicca — has specific protocols, holy days, practices, initiatory rites, spells, incantations, prayers and more. What to do, how to do it, who to do it with and when to do it is all spelled out (pardon the pun).

Not so with Christian Witchcraft. We have no handbook, no specific tradition, no rules. no dogma, no doctrine and no established do's and don'ts.

Though it's not new (I view Christ as the original Christian Witch), it's not codified.

While this can be refreshing to a creative Witch such as myself, I acknowledge that the non-codified nature of Christian Witchcraft (as it stands in 2020) can also be a little overwhelming to a beginner who has no idea where to start. As more and more Christian Witches emerge, more resources will be available.

Hence this book.

While this book is not here to codify being a Christian Witch, it's offered as an example of how you might codify your personal path, or not. Not everyone requires a code, or modus operandi. Not everyone requires instructions. Some of us flat out bristle at dogma and will have no parts of it. This is my camp. I left religion because it was stifling. I'm not about to form another religion.

I do, however, have protocols, practices, rituals, spells, prayers and more that feed my Christian Witchcraft and thus, my soul.

You could do this on your own. It will take years. But then again, what else are we going to be up to anyway? Any kind of magickal path takes years, if not decades, to master.

An excellent question to ask oneself is: am I going to go it alone? Or am I going to partner up with a gaggle of Christian Witches like me?

Though I don't yet belong to a coven, I'm almost completely certain that I will form one as led and inspired sometime in the future. This decision is informed by the Christian Witches Mystery School in which we get to practice magick together in class. It's lovely. I revel in the shared energy of a bunch of bad-a magickal Witches, Wizards and Warlocks.

On the other side of the proverbial coin of 'shared energy' is the possibility of exposure to funky energy (more on this later).

If we're lawful, we remember that we cannot experience on the outside what does not have a correspondence on the inside. Whatever is in front of me somehow landed there because an aspect of me summoned it. Yes, it may have been a rogue aspect of me, yet I summoned it nonetheless, a fact that I take particular joy in because it reminds me of my ultimate power. It also holds me accountable to what shows up in my life.

Coven or solitary? You choose. What I know is that on this path, a coven could be particularly helpful when it comes to you establishing your practices and protocols. There's a shared pool of wisdom and knowledge in a coven that is both uncanny and unparalleled.

If you choose to join or form a Christian Witches Coven, you may find the chapter on Coven Formation helpful as inspiration.

Decisions

You will face a multiplicity of decisions as a Christian Witch, far more than I can write about in one volume.

More important than the decisions you make is the inner space from which you make those decisions. This equates to your true intention.

I created a decision making tool that would guide me in the direction of my soul... my highest aspirations and calling, above the fray of the surface egoic mind, far beyond any perceived confusion. I named the tool the *Gauntlet for Decision Making*. It contains 8 simple questions. I first wrote it out in a grimoire years ago (it's published in the resources section of my book **Confessions of a Christian Witch**). I've used it ceaselessly. It has never failed me.

If you don't use this tool, I would recommend that you create your own tool by which you are CERTAIN you are acting with and from the True Will when making decisions.

We can never be too careful about the place within where our decision-making is originating. If our decisions are being made from an inner fearful place, fear will result. This is not a question, or a maybe. This is law.

If your decisions are being made from love, then you'll receive love outcomes. This doesn't mean love outcomes are always pleasing. They're not. Some of the most loving things the universe serves up to us are the most displeasing.

The beauty is, you have the ultimate power in your life: the power of **CHOICE**. This is what makes you **SOVEREIGN**.

Now let's move on to the next phase of this book: your declaration.

II

DECLARE

Your declaration is a power statement.
Let's go...

What is a Declaration?

A declaration is defined as "a formal or explicit statement or announcement" or "the formal announcement of the beginning of a state or condition."

Because I'm a Christian Witch who loves reading the Bible, I'll share a favorite scripture:

"In the beginning was the Word, and the Word was with God, and the Word was God." - 1 John 1:1 (KJV)

This message teaches the energetic creative action and power of the Word (with a capital W).

Some churches teach that this verse refers to Christ. Maybe it does. Maybe it doesn't. That's not what we're discussing here. What we're discussing here is the immense and precise creative power in the WORD. When you speak a thing, that thing is being created through a process governed by law.

WORDS BECOME THINGS.

This is a magickal maxim. Every magickal and/or occult tradition relies heavily upon and enthusiastically utilizes the potent power of WORDS in the form of invocations, incantations, spells, evocations, prayers and more, with many rituals requiring laser accuracy with the WORDS expressed, while others require exact arrangement and placement of each WORD.

Why is so much care devoted to WORDS?

It goes without saying that every one of us has experienced the mighty effects of the spoken word.

As a practicing Christian Witch, you can now put this power to good use by making a **DECLARATION** of who you are and what you do. In church, people make declarations of faith. At the altar, partners make vows of togetherness and love. Same concept.

You have the wonderful and sublime opportunity to make a formal and explicit statement or announcement that you are now a Christian Witch. You can make a formal announcement of the beginning of a new state of being and doing for yourself.

This becomes your initiation, should you choose to have one. While initiatory rites as a Christian Witch will be offered later in this tome, it deserves a word or two here as well.

Initiation involves the WORD. Initiates, in many traditions, are required to speak WORDS, or make a confession of some sort. Some rites require a statement of renunciation, while others require a positive affirmation of what will be done going forward.

Because an initiation is binding, as are words (unless or until they're canceled) the two work seamlessly together in magickal tradition after magickal tradition to bind the initiate to the path by invoking the vast resources of the unconscious. This is especially true in initiations, rituals or practices where a phrase is oft repeated. These WORDS become mnemonic devices, solidifying the initiate on the path even when unforeseen circumstances would normally cause one to waver.

We cannot overstate the power of WORDS, hence the power of your DECLARATION. Let's take a look at a sample.

The Declaration

Here is a simple, sample Declaration that can be utilized in a Christian Witch's initiation. This Declaration is also included in the example Initiatory Order of Rites in this book:

DECLARATION

I, __*Kayla Murphy*__ (state your name here) do hereby declare and solemnly swear that I am called to be a Christian Witch.

I answer this call of my soul with all I have and all I am.
From the core of my being, and with every ounce of my breath I say YES!

I take this vow wholeheartedly, without coercion from any outside force. This decision and resulting declaration is fully and unequivocally my own.

I DECLARE I will study to show myself approved.
I DECLARE I will regard my soul first.
I DECLARE I will love and stand on inner knowing first and foremost, beyond any outside influences, no matter how close to me these may be.

I DECLARE I will use the WORD of GOD aright.

I DECLARE I will walk in the LIGHT, guided by the Luminosity of God/Goddess/I AM.

I DECLARE I practice magick with complete alignment with the divine will.
I DECLARE I uphold, live by, deeply regard and honor the Witch's Code: to know, to will, to dare, to keep silent.

I DECLARE I uphold, love, support and root for all those in the magickal community.
I DECLARE I aspire to be a light to my coven mates, and an inspiration to all.
When they see me, they see Source.
Where ever I go, and whatever I may be doing, I vow to bring peace and never dissension.

I DECLARE I uphold and live by the laws of the ancient Hermetic Arts & Sciences.
I DECLARE I regard magick as the Great Work and I take on this Alchemy of the Soul wholeheartedly.

I DECLARE all is well with my soul, and all will always be well with my soul.
I DECLARE I am a healer and I choose to use these healing powers for the fulfillment of divine perfection for all, including humans, animals, nature and beings who are not in flesh.

I DECLARE I am a teacher who gladly shares TRUTH.
I DECLARE I am a WISDOM KEEPER who gladly shares my experiences as inspired.

I DECLARE nothing I see is bigger than me.
I DECLARE I am first and foremost committed to the Higher Self, my Holy Guardian Angel, the Light of my Soul and the Keeper of my Life. This Eternal Flame that is God/Goddess as me is the ONLY AND FINAL

The Declaration

AUTHORITY in my world.

I DECLARE the WORD is a lamp unto my feet and a light unto my path.
I DECLARE I am protected, guarded, guided, richly provided for, watched over, doted upon, adored, cheered on and made whole, perfect and rich in every way by this delicious Universe of Life!

I DECLARE I AM A CHRISTIAN WITCH AND NOW UNDERTAKE TO DO ALL IN MY POWER TO UPLIFT THIS PATH WITH LOVE, GRACE, TRUTH, POWER AND DIVINE BEAUTY!
I DECLARE CHRIST IS MY HIGHEST IDEAL!
I DECLARE I AM ONE WITH THE ONE!

AMEN
ASE
SO MOTE IT BE

To Whom Are You Making the Declaration?

YOU.

You are making the declaration to *yourself*.

There's nothing in the definition of a declaration that says it has to be public, yet a connotation exists of a soap box, or a megaphone.

No megaphones required.

This is about YOU, for YOU.

You can 100% trust that if the declaration is truly made to yourself, it's also made to everyone around you.

Conversely, if you didn't truly make a declaration to yourself within yourself, it doesn't matter what you shout from the rooftops, no one will believe you.

You may wonder about the power of making a declaration to yourself.

The power is closely related to your power of choice.

When you make a silent vow within yourself — that's held to be in alignment with the truth of who you are — you know the unshakable power of that decision.

We've done this a million times. We've made some silent decision within self, about something deeply important, usually on the heels of some horrific contrast. We may have spoken it under the breath in a hushed tone. "This will never happen again." There was an inner decision, followed by the power of the WORD.

The result? You've never had that thing happen again. The universe heard you. It's always listening.

This is the power of the silent vow, the declaration to one's Self.

I'm not suggesting that you will never make a declaration to anyone else about you being a Christian Witch. Indeed, your initiation may be full of coven mates and/or magickal friends and family.

I'm saying that the first declaration about you being a Christian Witch must be made to ***yourself, within yourself.***

Without this first solid, sincere, unshakable declaration to Self, all else is moot.

No one can seek to go out and claim to be in the world — with credibility — what they have not solidified and indeed ***become*** within their own heart and soul.

Now let's go deeper into initiation.

Initiation as a Christian Witch

~~~~~

An initiation into this path is not required in order to be a practicing Christian Witch, yet it can be powerful. The initiation is where you will make your Declaration. If you choose not to have an initiation, you can make your Declaration to yourself in a private ritual.

If you choose to have an initiation, it can be a solitary affair in nature or in your sacred space in your home, or it can be done with your Christian Witches Coven at a temple or other appropriate location. You get to choose, from deep within your soul.

Only you know what's right for you.

Before we go into the specifics of initiation, let's explore the definition a tiny bit.

Initiation Definition

Definitions of initiation found online include:

- "the action of admitting someone into a secret or obscure society or group, typically with a ritual"
- "the action of beginning something"
- "the rites, ceremonies, ordeals, or instructions with which one is made a member of a sect or society or is invested with a particular function or

status"
- "the condition of being initiated into some experience or sphere of activity"

The Trap

What we know is that initiation is a beginning point, not a completion point.

This is critical to remember as a Christian Witch so that no bloating occurs. A very real trap in magick is megalomania and delusions of grandeur.

Megalomania is defined as "obsession with the exercise of power, especially in the domination of others" and "delusion about one's own power or importance (typically as a symptom of manic or paranoid disorder)."

Why is this a very real trap? Because magick puts us in contact and working relationship with vast power and powers (spirits). In a consciousness that's not 100% committed to humility, servant leadership and Christ-hood (the scriptures at Matthew 20:25-27, Matthew 23:11, Mark 9:33-35 and Mark 10:42-44 come to mind), there's a very real possibility of arrogance taking root and/or destruction by pride.

"Pride goeth before destruction, and an haughty spirit before a fall." - Proverbs 16:18 (KJV)

While I'm sure no one is becoming initiated with an intention of taking over Christian Witches everywhere, unacknowledged issues that lie dormant in the vast well of the unconscious can be awakened by magick. When shadow energies begin to surface because of our spiritual practices (which is normal and expected), if we do not take the golden opportunity to address and integrate these, a gargantuan problem can arise. Shadow work — with the intention of self-mastery — will prevent pride, arrogance, narcissism, megalomania and destroying oneself from the inside out (more on shadow work is coming up in Part 4). One of the best resources on the planet for shadow work is the new book by a fave witch of mine Carolyn Elliott, titled ***Existential Kink: Unmask Your Shadow and Embrace Your Power***.

We do well to keep humility at the forefront and continually engage in shadow work.

How to Be a Christian Witch — Helena "shining light"

For me, humility is a protection. One of my sacred names (more on your new name later in this tome) is Shona Ife, which means humility and love. When I received the name, it came with a charge:

RISE TO THE ESSENCE OF YOUR NAME!

Wow.

That was mind-blowing.

Ok.

Um... how do I do that?

It's been over a decade and I'm still working on it. Humility, for me, is a life-long spiritual aspiration. Arrogance is so automatic and the ego so insidious that we literally must be on guard. I don't mean being tense or uptight about it. We get to **BE AWARE**. Self-awareness leads to self-mastery.

After awareness dawns, simply course correct in the moment. That's all. See the arrogance, or the ego playing out dreams of grandeur, then CORRECT. This is all that's required. Never beat yourself up because pride or arrogance nipped at your heels. It's trying to get all of us, trust me.

How do we become aware? You can always tell when you're going off the rails by **presence in the moment**. How do you feel? Does it feel good? How's your breathing? What's happening in your body?

I can always tell when I go off the rails because I don't feel peaceful. Since peace of mind is all important to me, I seek to practice, as best I can, being peaceful. Blissful even. When my peace is disturbed, it's an opportunity for me to look at myself (not others).

How do we correct? Intention. I hold life intentions to be LOVE, to live according to the 7 Hermetic Laws and the 9 Fruit of the Spirit (Galatians 5:22-23). I describe this in detail in my book **Christian Witches Manifesto**. When my ego has made a grab for the steering wheel, and I feel the disturbance in my energetic system, I get to remind myself that I already chose. I chose love. I chose humility. Now I get to remember my choice and put it into effect **IN THE MOMENT**.

It's simple, when we make it a practice.

Is it easy? No. It gets easier the more we practice, so we practice, practice, practice. This is the essence of self-mastery: being aware of what's going on

Peaceful

~ Choose Love everytime. Love wins.

with self in any given moment, and choosing how to think, feel, speak and act. This is responsibility: the ability to choose a response.

The good news about this process: no strikes go against us if pride or arrogance gets us, as long as we become AWARE in the moment, and transform by choosing humility instead. There are, however, heavy learning corrections if the universe has to do it for us because we're not aware. The universe will keep presenting us with opportunities to become AWARE, and to TRANSFORM.

A good question to meditate on is: what is humility? It's easy to have a skewed idea of what humility is due to conditioning. Even the dictionary defines humility as "a modest or low view of one's own importance." This is not a definition I agree with.

The wires were crossed (in my mind) between humility and self-debasement. These are not the same. I had it twisted and thought humility meant being last, letting other people walk all over me, tamping down my desires and dreams as if they weren't important, not being forward and/or not readily speaking up, as well as all manner of dysfunctional attitudes and behavior that invite unloving (or even abusive) relationships.

That is NOT humility.

Humility contains the root word 'humus' meaning 'of the earth.'

Humility carries, for me, a knowing that I am of the earth, and a reminder to stay grounded and rooted in truth, no matter how much success is experienced. Humility aligns with the spiritual principle of equanimity, that all are equal (not the same, simply equal). We're all different. We get to celebrate our differences, not use them as ego food to feel better than or less than anyone else.

Stay grounded and rooted in truth, and you'll be fine. If you're leading a coven, be ever mindful to be a servant leader. Christ did the foot washing for everyone present. This bears remembering so that we enter this journey with the appropriate mindset, and can quickly course correct when we have human moments, which we all will.

I envision the rootedness of humility symbolized in nature as trees. Trees are completely rooted, with the tallest, most sturdy trees having the deepest, most intricate root system. The only means by which a tree can stretch to the heavens is because it's roots go deep into the earth. Without rootedness in the Earth Mother, there's no stretching toward the sky. I like to use this analogy to stay in 'tree' mind: ever deepening roots (humility) while simultaneously stretching to the sky (aspiration).

Consider the hubris of Icarus as a cautionary tale. Those who are seeking power over others will soon meet with folly. All power is within. Expressing it in loving ways that serve others is the truth of why we're here. If you dive deep into the power within and effectively, continually, creatively and fully express this power, rather than attempt to control or power grab on the outside, self-mastery begins to dawn. With ever increasing self-mastery comes the award of greater power and responsibility. You've earned it.

Now that the warning has been issued, let's move on to initiation considerations.

Initiation Considerations

Remember, all of the information here constitute ideas and offerings. You get to choose all the elements offered in any section of this book, or some of the elements, or none of the elements. It's a buffet. You choose what to eat.

You can utilize these ideas as an inspirational springboard to create your own initiation with all of your own self-created, hand-crafted, deeply personal elements, rituals, prayers and attire… all created by you, for you. That would be magnificent.

Study of Magickal Systems

As we've established, initiation is a starting point and not an arrival point. I encourage you to study the initiatory processes, protocols and grades among magickal systems and traditions around the world, especially:

- O.T.O. (Ordo Templi Orientis) - the O.T.O. is Aleister Crowley's magickal legacy.

- The Hermetic Order of the Golden Dawn - one of my all-time fave books on the Golden Dawn system of magick is **The Essential Golden Dawn** by Chic Cicero and Sandra Tabatha Cicero. (FYI, this book is currently listed for an exorbitant price on Amazon, so see if you can find it in a book shop that specializes in old or rare books or in a magick/metaphysical shop.) You can also read Israel Regardie's book **The Golden Dawn**.
- Enochian Vision Magick - while not an initiatory system of magick, it's still quite compelling to study and practice. The Enochian Calls are keys which give immediate access and entry into multi-dimensional experiences, if engaged appropriately. One of my best recommendations is Lon Milo Duquette's book **Enochian Vision Magick** (which I've had more magick with than I anticipated).
- Solomonic or Ceremonial Magick - though there is no one protocol or system for practicing Solomonic Magick, it's worth studying to understand the principles and underlying laws of magick, particularly with regard to summoning spirits. Esoteric Archives carries a considerable number of the older grimoires that detail ceremonial magick and Solomonic rituals.

Be careful with any and all systems of magick. You're engaging potent energies and powerful spirits. Just as you've learned the operating laws of other potent energies, such as fire, electricity and sexual energy, you'll be required to do the same in magick in order to become a master.

A Word About Timing

With the intention to manage expectations on the magickal path, I offer that you remember:

- All magickal systems and/or traditions require YEARS to master.
- Initiatory grades of many magickal systems require YEARS to accomplish.
- Some initiatory grades are by invitation only, which means the initiate

must prove mastery in the lodge before being asked and sponsored to move to higher grades.

In short, no magickal initiation is instant, so don't rush. Magickal mastery is measured in years and decades, not weeks or months. Give your life to accomplishing the Great Work.

Initiation Grades

Grades in initiatory magickal systems are levels of magickal and spiritual mastery that must be DEMONSTRATED in one's life, and are not dependent upon paperwork or knowledge. There are plenty of people who can spout magickal information until the cows come home, yet their life is in shambles. This is NOT mastery.

Though Christian Witchcraft is not a system of magick that requires grades, we do well to consider a few of the terms for grades that exist in magickal systems around the globe, and can be loosely applied to what we do in Christian Witchcraft. If for no other reason, it gives us a map of where we're going, and can provide a means of helping others in our covens and communities along on their magickal path.

To keep it simple, I'm condensing magickal grades, which find correspondences in many systems of magick, into 5 broad ranges here (though some magickal systems may have as many as a dozen or more grades). These 5 broad ranges are:

- Neophyte - brand new to magick, knowing little or nothing. Believe it or not, this is a beautiful place to be! There's a completely open, blank slate on which to create your magickal path. Celebrate!
- Aspirant - a student who's still at the starting point of the magickal system, yet has soul-searched and learned enough to know that they're ready to commit to initiation. Likely, there will be a calling from spirit realms, or one's 'head spirit' (such as an Orisha) will supernaturally lead the aspirant in the direction of initiation. The aspirant's main 2-fold

focus is to: study and prepare oneself for initiation. Some systems require a 1-year period to appropriately prepare for initiation.
- Initiate - one who is initiated, and now is deeper in study, is practicing the basics of the magickal system and is being inducted into the deeper mysteries.
- Mage/Magus - one who is a master of magick and has achieved — among other magickal feats — Knowledge and Conversation of the Holy Guardian Angel (known as K&C of the HGA, or simply K&C for short, more on this below), the Philosopher's Stone (a term from alchemy referring to the ability to transform base metals into gold on the physical plane, and on the spiritual plane, the ability to transform one's base animal nature into the pure gold of Spirit). Mage indicates a level of spiritual and magickal mastery that is indeed rare.
- Grand Mage/Magus - one who is beyond all grades and all earthly considerations. An enlightened being, such as a Christ or a Buddha.

This gives a flexible outline of what we're working toward, and can serve as a road map.

Grades of Initiation in the Covenant of Christian Witches Mystery School

In the Covenant of Christian Witches Mystery School (CCW), which was founded in October 2018 at our first ever classes held in Salem, Massachusetts, there are 3 initiatory grades in the first phase.

Please note that the initiatory grades in the Mystery School are NOT the same as initiation as a Christian Witch.

All aspects of your initiation as a Christian Witch are completely up to you and your creative and intuitive knowing.

In the Mystery School, there are set grades. These are:

- **Hermetic** - all students begin in the Mystery School as a Hermetic, which is simply one who **STUDIES** and **APPLIES** the Magickal Arts & Sciences of the Western Esoteric tradition passed down to us from Egypt. Hermes is the father of the Western Esocteric school of magick. In the Mystery School, the Hermetic must complete all 40 classes in the **FOUNDATIONS** course of study, and successfully *demonstrate* these in one's life before applying for initiation. Foundations classes include introduction to Christian Witchcraft, Hermetic Law, Bible Magick, Angelology, Demonology, Spell Crafting, Divination and more. The word *demonstrate*, in this context, means that the evidence of having integrated these 40 lessons is present in the student's life and affairs. In short, your life should be getting noticeably better if you're applying what you've learned. The Mystery School is not about passing tests on paper. It's about passing tests in one's life.

- **Hierophant** - after one is initiated in the Mystery School, this person is known as a Heirophant (from the Tarot). At this grade, the Initiate is engaged in rigorous daily spiritual practice to achieve Knowledge & Conversation of the Holy Guardian Angel (K&C of the HGA), which is about a 6-month magickal operation. Knowledge and Conversation of the Holy Guardian Angel means you've conjured the tangible, visceral presence of your Holy Guardian Angel through daily rigorous practices that include ritual purity and prayer, and have received the name of this Angel, and have entered into a sacred intimate relationship with this visceral presence in every aspect of your life and every sphere of activity such that you know exactly what to do at all times. Some refer to the Holy Guardian Angel as the Higher Self. I like to think of the HGA as a 'head spirit,' not unlike the Orishas in Yoruba. I go into more detail about this in Tenet #1 of the 10 Tenets in the **Christian Witches Manifesto**.

- **High Priest/High Priestess/High Mage/High Witch/High Wizard** - after one has successfully achieved K&C of the HGA, this one becomes a High Priest or Priestess, or for those who prefer gender neutral terms: a High Mage, High Witch or High Wizard. This one is a spiritually mature, magickal master who is in total and complete surrender to the will of the divine as the True Self, is manifesting destiny (True Will) on the earth plane, is engaged in the work of global transformation appropriate to one's gifting, abilities and capabilities, and is a beacon for the coven, Christian Witches global community and the magickal community at large. This one has given one's life to the spiritual calling of becoming a **Christ**.

I share a little of the Mystery School with you here to provide greater clarity, and to spark ideas and inspiration for visioning and mapping your magickal path.

Initiation Privacy & Safety Precautions

Before we go into more detail, as a general rule, please remember the usual precautions:

Privacy is monumental! Do NOT perform any initiatory rituals around normal people! You may scare the bejesus out of them, which is not the intention. Keep everything highly private. If you're working outdoors, do as Christ did when engaging in spiritual practices: he retreated to a lonely place.

Be safe! Take good care of yourself. Be careful around flames, and especially mind your robes near candles. Be careful around river banks and oceans, especially if you don't swim, or don't swim well. Many rituals are done at night. If it's dark and no one is with you, it goes without saying that you ought to be in a place you are certain is SAFE (not only with regard to people; consider that there may be wild animals afoot, in their natural habitat). Your back yard may even be an option.

Let someone know where you are. If you're doing a solitary initiation, trust in someone who's like-minded and let them know where you're going for your initiation and how long (approximately) it could take. Check in with them when you return to let them know you're home safe and all is well.

Have a partner, teacher or coven mates with you. If you feel led, invite others to your initiation. If you're a member of a coven, then the coven most likely will be present. If you're not a member of a coven, then inviting other witchy friends could make for a richer experience. If you're not in a coven and don't have witchy friends, consider having someone from the Christian Witches community support you (search for and build relationships with other Christian Witches you've met online). Whomever you choose to invite, make sure all individuals who accompany you are magickal and like minded. ~~Energy is infectious and the person with the strongest energy wins.~~

Next, let's take a closer look at the blood oath.

[Handwritten note: Energy is infectious the person with the strongest energy wins]

The Blood Oath

~·~

Many initiations around the world involve blood, either that of the initiate, or of an animal.

Allow me for a moment to reflect on my visit to the Masai village on the African plains of Kenya. The village chief's son explained to us the process used to extract blood from the neck vein of a cow by using a straw (it doesn't kill the cow) in order to let enough blood into a gourd for them to drink. I almost hurled right there and then.

Though the Masai are herders who do not kill cows, nor do they eat the flesh of cows, they drink the blood of cows to mark special or significant occasions. They also take care that the cow is not endangered nor does it die due to loss of blood in the process.

The Masai take blood very seriously. And for good reason.

Blood is potent. Blood is a pact binder. Blood is life. Blood is a deal maker, and a deal breaker. A blood oath is a binding oath for all eternity.

This is why we use a blood oath in initiations.

For those who are squeamish about the issue, remember that when anyone arrives at the doctor's office for a checkup, they're not in the door for 15 minutes before they've been disrobed and relieved of urine and a couple of tubes of blood. Why? Because the scientist can examine the patient's blood to determine the condition of the body.

We have no problem with these procedures. We do not object. We even think blood-letting at the hands of a doctor is normal.

Women who are in the 1st and 2nd phases of the Goddess' triple aspects (maiden, mother, crone) may have a blood flow cycle that coincides with the moon. Babies are born amidst blood.

When we were kids, you may have become 'blood brothers' (or sisters or otherwise) with a good friend in a ceremony of sorts where you both let blood and mixed it.

To normalize initiatory blood, realize that the amount of blood that will leave your body for a blood oath is considerably less than what a doctor drains you of in a routine examination, with no untoward effects.

I'm not saying to slit wrists or cut a vein. We absolutely would NOT ever do that in magick. In the initiation, we speak of using a blade of some sort to draw blood. You can just as easily (and I've used this method when initiating others as well) prick your thumb with a pin and squeeze blood out. The amount of blood is not the issue. A drop of blood will do.

I'd like to state at this juncture that the blood oath has its precedent in the Bible. A solemn oath was often sealed with animal blood of some kind. Passover is such a tradition. With that said, there are scriptures in the Bible that speak of using blood to seal an oath between God and humankind, or to cleanse 'sins' or for sacrifices for a multitude of reasons. The use of blood in a spiritual and/or religious context (see Exodus 29:21) is not strange or unusual.

If you don't feel comfortable with a blood oath, don't do it.

If you do feel comfortable with it, proceed in a safe manner.

Proceed Safely

Remember these precautions in order to proceed in a safe manner.

EVERYONE WORKS EXCLUSIVELY WITH THEIR OWN BLOOD. We do not touch blood that belongs to other people and we do not give other people our blood.

When making a pin prick, be sure to burn the tip of the pin with a lighter, over a flame or candle to disinfect before use. Alcohol can be used as well. If using your personal knife, dagger or athame, be sure it's clean and disinfected before making the small cut. I think this goes without saying, but I'll state it anyway: everyone uses their own personal pin or knife, with no sharing.

After the pin prick or cut, be sure to keep your hand away from surfaces, people and/or dirt. Keep the cut clean.

Procuring Blood for the Declaration

The blood oath is made by pricking a finger (or making a small cut with a dagger in the palm of the hand making sure to avoid veins) and sealing a written oath by pressing the finger to the page so that the blood is on the page, in a precise spot, similar to a signature.

If a small cut is made, the hand can be placed face down and rubbed on a non-porous surface, such as a rock, to cover the entire surface of the hand in blood. A hand print is then applied to your initiation document. Blood coagulates fairly quickly, so move with intention. After the ritual, the blood rock can be kept to take home and place on your altar, or it can be washed clean with fresh running water and returned to nature. DO NOT LEAVE YOUR BLOOD PRINT ON A ROCK SOMEWHERE.

Another choice could be to use menstrual blood for the occasion.

In some circles, including in the Hebrew Bible, menstrual blood is considered unclean. When I visit Bali, which I do frequently as it's my soul home, I love to go to the temples. Bali is a lunar society so the full moon temple celebrations bring tears to my eyes. The temples in Bali do not allow women to enter who are in moon time (menstruating).

The same is true for the Lakota Sweat Lodges I've been blessed to attend. Women in moon time do not enter. The Lakota say that a woman in moon time is so powerful that she will have an effect on the sweat lodge and everyone in it. The sweat lodge in Peru with a Shaman I love, Kush, had no such requirements.

Among witches, menstrual blood is sacred, a sign of the Goddess and fertility. Most of the witches I know are not squeamish about blood, and have no problem chasing a chicken or doing whatever else (legal of course) that may be required involving blood to get the job done.

Across the African diaspora in the U.S., it's well known that slave women who were forced to cook for cruel masters often put menstrual blood in the food. I've also heard anecdotally that the Obeah men in Jamaica may advise a woman to discreetly feed menstrual blood to a man she desires to keep in a 'love potion' of sorts.

While blood treatment and treatment of women in moon time varies across traditions, there's a constant: moon time blood flow is recognized as powerful, powerful enough to warrant considerations, specific protocols and even an honored place in spellwork.

If menstrual blood is the choice, keep timing in mind, especially if you desire fresh blood. Moon time is a potent time when the womb and the moon express their alignment. It's also a time when the body acknowledges it has not been impregnated and can shed any preparations for a baby, so this is rich blood. I had a childbirth coach for my first child who used to say that period flow was comprised of "the bloody tears of a disappointed uterus."

Because the moon regulates the flow of all water on planet earth, and the flow of menses, using period blood is a way to anchor lunar energies in the initiation (as opposed to, or in addition to solar energies). This can be powerful, especially if one's sign is Cancer, which is ruled by the moon.

The other upside to using menstrual blood is that no pin pricks or cuts are required. There's a natural flow of potent energy from the womb that can be tapped and added to your initiation Declaration that you'll keep for all time. How powerful is that!

It's simple to bring a menstrual blood soaked pad or cloth to the initiation (placed in a water proof, airtight container with a lid), or to use a menstrual cup for the collection of blood. I have not been able to master menstrual cups without getting blood in more places than desirable upon extraction, so I would opt for the blood soaked pad, but that's just me.

Place the palm of your hand face down on the pad and press. Slightly roll your fingers so that each finger is bloody, as well as the palm so that you're sure to get a good hand print on your Declaration. I've used the menstrual blood soaked pad approach, and it worked flawlessly.

The Blood Oath

If you're good with the use of a menstrual cup, extract the blood and pour it into a small, airtight container that will be sealed and placed in a refrigerator until time for use. If other people have access to your refrigerator: **MAKE SURE NO ONE COMES INTO CONTACT WITH YOUR BLOOD.** If you're using this method, collect the blood in the moon time cycle closest to your initiation. The blood will not stay liquefied in the fridge forever.

When using the collected menstrual blood during the initiation, simply pour it on one hand and smooth over your entire palm and fingers for the hand print. I've heard of some witches using a drop or two of alcohol to make sure the blood doesn't coagulate, but I've never used this method. See what works best for you.

A third option would be to use your own dried blood. I've read about this, though I've never tried it. The idea is to collect your blood, and spread a thin layer of it on a non-porous surface for it to dry. Once dried, it can be flaked off, ground with a pestle and mortar and preserved in an airtight bottle with a seal. The flakes can be used in potions of all sorts. If you opt to use this approach for the blood oath, keeping dried blood flakes is a lot easier to pull off than keeping liquid blood in the refrigerator. The blood flakes will have to be re-hydrated for the initiation, which can be accomplished by adding water. (A video of how to re-hydrate blood flakes is here on YouTube.)

Of the 3 methods listed here for procuring blood, my preference is drawing blood in the moment. It's freshest and purest. If you're actually in moon time while you're being initiated, using the fresh blood flow in the moment is even more potent.

Once the bloody hand print has been applied to your Declaration, it may take a few minutes to dry, especially if humid. Allow time for the Declaration to sit on the altar afterward (you'll see more about this in the initiation instructions).

Whenever I look at the page that contains my menstrual blood hand print, I remember just how potent and powerful a witch I truly am. I pray it does the same for you.

An aside that may border on a T.M.I. (too much information) violation is that as I write the menstrual blood portion of this blood oath chapter, a copious stream of menstrual blood is pouring from me. I find this experience utterly fascinating and quite magickal.

To conclude, as stated above, the amount of blood used is not as big a factor as the use of blood itself. Everyone alive has blood, so a blood oath is a universal ritual that anyone can perform. When it comes to your blood oath, trust yourself. You'll know what to do.

If you've written out your Declaration and sealed it with your blood fingerprint or hand print, you can roll it up (in scroll fashion), wrap it with a silk ribbon or swath of natural fiber fabric (silk is a natural fiber, as is pure cotton or wool, just remember everything is energy, so the origins of the fabric will play a role here), and place it in safe keeping (a place where you keep all your highly charged magickal items). Tell no one where you placed your blood-bound oath. MAKE SURE NO ONE EVER TOUCHES IT PHYSICALLY.

If desired, you can bring the Declaration out each year on the anniversary of your initiation to perform a Ritual of Remembrance (more on this later) to commemorate and deepen your commitment to being a Christian Witch.

Now let's take a look at your birth information.

Your Birth Code

Your entry point into this 3rd dimensional reality was carefully selected and orchestrated by your soul and Source. NOTHING about your birth, including timing and location, was random.

Since the soul took great care to determine the date, time and circumstances of birth, we must conclude that birth information is invaluable to the spiritual path and thus, one's ultimate destiny.

Here are the 6 pieces of birth information I find vitally important, and have been teaching on my YouTube channel for years:

Galactic Signature

Ever since I first discovered Galactic Signatures and Mayan Astrology over 13 years ago in a full moon circle with Manifest Ra in Washington, DC, I've been entranced.

I have not found a system of astrology that so thoroughly speaks to my soul and reads me in every direction like the Galactic Signature and the Fifth Force Oracle.

I realize that this may sound like Greek, so I'll offer 2 resources to start you off on this most delicious and compelling path. First, decode yourself by discovering your Galactic Signature based on your date of birth here: https://lawoftime.org/decode/.

After decoding yourself by receiving your Galactic Signature, type the result into a new browser window. For instance, I am kin 234: White Cosmic Wizard, so I'll open a browser and type in the words 'White Cosmic Wizard.'

The first result should be a full reading from Astro Dream Advisor on that particular Galactic Signature. Read the full page and take careful notes in your grimoire. This is your soul speaking to you.

I would also recommend that you completely commit to memory the 5 or 6 line mantra that accompanies your Galactic Signature. Meditate on it. It's contains keys to your destiny.

Numerology

The numerology of your birth is easy to determine. Simply add all the numbers of your birth date to arrive at a single digit. If the number you reduce to is a master number (11, 22, 33, 44, 55, 66 and so on), then rather than your birth number reading as one single digit, it would read as the master number, followed by the single digit.

For example, a person born on January 1, 1964 would calculate their birth number as follows: 1 + 1 + 1 + 9 + 6 + 4 = 22. In numerology, we would normally continue reducing the numbers until arriving at 1 single digit, for instance 2 + 2 = 4.

Yet, since the first number is a master number (22), this person's birth number would be 22/4.

As another point of consideration, the entire universe is mathematical, and there's a whole book in the Bible dedicated to numbers. Discovering the hidden messages in numbers is another critical element of the Magickal Arts & Sciences.

Tarot Birth Cards

Your Tarot Birth Cards are the Major Arcana cards corresponding to your birth number.

A Tarot Birth Card Calculator is online at the **Tarot School**. Simply enter your date of birth and the cards will pop up. You will either have 2 or 3 Tarot Birth Cards, depending upon the numerology of your birth. For instance, in the example used above, a person with the birth number 22/4 would have the following Tarot Birth Cards: The Emperor (Key #4) and the Death card (Key #13, which reduces to the number 4).

Those who are born under the number 1 will have 3 Tarot Birth Cards: The Magician (Key #1), the Wheel of Fortune (Key #10, which reduces to the number 1) and the Sun (Key #19, which also reduces to the number 1).

Once you've determined your Tarot Birth Cards, sleep with each card under your pillow for 7-10 days. Journal daily on the cards during this process in your grimoire. These specific cards hold a significant wealth of information for your soul's journey.

Western Astrology

Here we give attention to our sun sign, moon sign, rising sign and North Node. If you have a gifted astrologer you trust, invest in a full horoscope, including all your houses. I'm not big on Western Astrology, yet I know enough to be dangerous. More importantly, I know that the most critical element is to understand its role in my soul's unfoldment.

Eastern Astrology

In the west, we're not usually exposed to a great deal of Eastern Astrology, yet I've found it to be extremely useful. I delved deep into Eastern Astrology in my Feng Shui days, when it felt like I devoured every book I could find on the topic, especially books by **Lillian Too**. It was during this period that I came to have a deep and profound appreciation for all things Eastern Astrology, the elements in the east and Feng Shui.

In Eastern Astrology, we find the animal for the year in which we were born. For instance, I was born in the year of the ox. Then, we locate the element associated with our birth animal. For instance, the element for me is metal.

In Feng Shui and Eastern Astrology, the elements vary from the Western Esoteric Tradition. They are:

- Fire
- Earth
- Metal
- Water
- Wood

Since there are 5 elements, there are 5 types of each animal in Eastern Astrology. For instance, there are 5 types of ox: fire ox, earth ox, metal ox, water ox and wood ox. The last digit in your birth year determines your element:

- Metal: Birth years ending in 0 or 1.
- Water: Birth years ending in 2 or 3.
- Wood: Birth years ending in 4 or 5.
- Fire: Birth years ending in 6 or 7.
- Earth: Birth years ending in 8 or 9.

Since the year of my birth ends with the number 1, I'm a metal ox in the Chinese Zodiac.

Use this information to meditate on, research, understand and apply in Feng Shui to usher in greater health, wealth, harmony, happiness and overall sense of well-being.

You can simply conduct a search for Chinese Astrology to easily find your animal and element.

Birthday Psalm

It came to me several years ago from the angelic realm that every person has a birthday Psalm. Mine is Psalm 34.

From the time I began revealing this information, there's been the same response from every person who hears it: how can I find mine?!?

I've asked, and have been still in order to receive a definitive answer to that question. It's been a little bit of a challenge. The angels haven't given me a clear cut process yet. There's good reason for this, so I'll share with you the process of how my birthday Psalm came to me as a ***knowing*** (do NOT guess).

Many years back, I received a divine assignment from Higher Self to read the entire book of Psalms. I'd been desperately praying about a gnarly issue in my life, and didn't have anything else to do that afternoon, so I was all in. There was a sense that I was on the verge of an answer.

Even still, there are 150 Psalms, so as you might imagine, it was quite the task.

That afternoon, I sat down and committed to not getting up until I had completed the reading of the entire book of Psalms. Of course, the usual resistance arose — as will be the case with any divine assignment that challenges the lower mind — including becoming sleepy all of a sudden, wanting a snack and having to go to the bathroom more than usual. Consider that and any number of tricks the egoic mind can come up with in an attempt to foil a divine assignment, and you'll know of what I speak.

I received inspiration to write every appearance in the book of Psalms of the word 'trust' or any of its synonyms (confidence, firm reliance, etc). I took out my journal and did exactly that.

When I completed the 150th Psalm, a blazing realization stood in my consciousness: there's an inseparable connection between TRUST and PRAISE. I had become privy to a secret I've never forgotten: those who trust have reason to praise, and those who praise, trust.

The other result of drinking the entire book of Psalms in one sitting was my next book. I wasn't planning to write a book when I took on the assignment. That was Spirit's next trick up its proverbial sleeve: in helping myself, I'd be helping others. The book born of the exercise was ***How to Trust: A Psalms Prayer Journal***.

There's more. Our community undertook a collective program called "Psalm-A-Day" in which we met at 4:44 AM each morning to pray, read one

Psalm and discuss it. I was the leading minister. Over the next approximately 6 months (150 days straight), we met each morning for a Psalm.

In the process of reading the entire book of Psalms, writing the Psalms prayer journal, and conducting Psalm-A-Day for our community, the knowledge of the birthday Psalm came to me.

Maybe it was due to immersion in the book of Psalms. All these events did not exactly happen together. They were on a continuum.

The angels were speaking to me. In the process my birthday Psalm was revealed to me, along with the revelation that everyone has a birthday Psalm.

I read Psalm 34 over and over, and still do. I go to it as a check up, to determine if my life aligns with the essence of the Psalm. I practice it. I aspire to live up to every verse. It has my entire destiny laid out. It's uncannily accurate on who I am and what I do in service to humanity.

Your birthday Psalm is akin to another key that unlocks the code of your destiny.

When a good friend of mine and I discussed this (she's a spiritual master), she instantly knew what her birthday Psalm was. So this process isn't hard. It's more of a function of intuition and alignment.

Considering the foregoing, it would be impossible for me to give you a linear process for discovering your birthday Psalm. Here's what I can offer you:

- Set your intention to discover your birthday Psalm.
- Pray on it.
- Trust that it will come to you in perfect divine timing.
- Set a date and prepare yourself to read the entire book of Psalms at one time. Reserve about 4+ hours for this holy endeavor, taking into consideration your personal reading pace and comprehension. Everyone's different. Make sure you're alone and undisturbed so you can engage each Psalm at the deepest level.
- Have your grimoire with you to note any Psalm that stands out to you, or is deeply personal to you, or that seems to be talking about your life.

If reading the entire book in one sitting does not reveal the birthday Psalm to you such that you have complete certainty, proceed to the next steps:

- By inspiration, select a time to read one Psalm a day for 150 days straight. We practiced at 4:44 AM. The number 444 is an angel number of unconditional love. The angels were leading the charge for us as we embraced a Psalm a day.
- Prepare with prayer before each day's reading. Remember your intention to receive your birthday Psalm as a key to the code that is your destiny. Have a clear glass of fresh water on the altar for clarity. Change the water daily before the reading.
- Read 1 Psalm daily at the same time (the time you selected by inspiration).
- Journal on it in your grimoire.

That's it. The birthday Psalm will likely become clear to you. If it doesn't, TRUST. IT WILL COME. We just don't know where, when or how. Isn't that the fun part? This is why the spiritual journey is called a mystery… and a glorious one at that!

Those are my top 6 when it comes to each soul's unique birth code. Use and integrate your birth information to decode any issues in your life, recurring or otherwise. Either your Galactic Signature, or your birth number(s), or your Tarot Birth Cards, or your Western Astrology, or your Chinese Zodiac, or your birthday Psalm, or any combination of the above, will provide answers.

I pray your birth code serves you well. There's an in-depth video about this on my YouTube channel titled: How to Decode Yourself with These 5 Aspects (sans the birthday Psalm information, fyi).

The Initiator

An Initiator is a person who has endured the trials of initiation and has proven worthy, has demonstrated mastery, and/or carries the magickal 'current' in the lineage of the magickal system or tradition involved. The 'current' referred to here is a stream of magickal energy transmitted from one person to the next.

No one owns this magickal current. As witches, we are conduits through which this magickal current flows.

During the initiation, this magickal current is transmitted from one who has been initiated to one who is being initiated.

There are many names and/or titles conferred upon those who have been initiated, as mentioned earlier. High Priests and/or High Priestesses are common terms, and to honor those who are not identified with any particular gender, a High Mage or High Warlock or High Witch or High Wizard are all suitable titles for an initiated Christian Witch. For me, the words witch, wizard and warlock are not gender specific (others may have a different view).

If you're performing a self-initiation, the magickal current is being bestowed upon and transmitted to you from above. This was my experience when I was first initiated as a witch in the early 2000's. I completed a self-initiation, in which I became aware that the magickal current was being transmitted from heavenly realms.

With that said, ***you do not ever need anyone else on your spiritual and/or magickal journey***. Other people are a beautiful addition to what you know you are called to be and do. Everything begins and ends with SELF. Beyond that, add all the community members and teachers you like.

It's important to understand the Initiator's role, on an energetic level. This person is initiated, so they can transmit the magickal current that's been transmitted to them. The Initiator also can act in an advisory role. You, the initiate, always INITIATE. You are the leader in the dance. **Never hand your power over to anyone outside yourself.**

To what degree you engage the knowledge, skill, wisdom, magickal mastery and expertise of the Initiator entirely depends upon you, your magickal prowess, your stage of development as a witch and more considerations that only your Higher Self will know.

The following is a list of responsibilities that an Initiator would be well able to handle. Ideally, the 2 of you will have had many discussions on what role the Initiator will play, as well as what you're asking of them, and in turn, what they're willing to provide. Here are a few possibilities of the responsibilities of an Initiator:

- Advising the initiate(s) on the clothing and/or robes, including specific colors, to be worn before, during and after initiation. In many instances, what an initiate wears before the initiation is not the same attire that will be worn during the initiation, or after the initiation. There are many reasons for this. One major reason is that the person who shows up for the initiation is not the same person who leaves the initiation. This is symbolized by changing of outer garments. If the initiate is a member of a coven, coven colors will likely be worn.
- Advising the initiate(s) of what supplies will be required for the initiation. (The following chapter offers a list of possibilities.)
- Advising the initiate(s) of the most auspicious day, date, time and hour of all initiatory rites. These have likely been calculated based on astrological influences, or angelic days and hours, and/or planetary days and hours, or to coincide with a lunar or solar event (such as a new moon or the fall

equinox, for instance). An Initiator who's knowledgeable in this arena is a great help, especially if the initiate is not.
- Advising the initiate(s) and all parties involved (such as coven members who will be present) of the order of the initiation. This is the official Initiatory Order of Rites (more on this coming up, as well as a sample). A written copy of this document is present at the initiation so that all involved are aware of each step and each role in the initiatory process. For instance, someone may be asked to offer a prayer, or read a Psalm, such as the 23rd Psalm. This will all be spelled out in the Initiatory Order of Rites.
- Preparing sacred space. Cleansing and purification of sacred space is a must before initiation. Definition of sacred space is critical. This may involve casting a circle to define where the initiation is taking place. If taking place in an indoor temple, or a cave for instance, parameters will be set to indicate where all rites and rituals will take place in the space. The angels will be called in (see below). Water and light can be placed at the 4 corners (see below). Consider all the ways you establish sacred space in your magickal workings. Elements will also be integrated in your initiation.
- Conducting the initiation. The Initiator will conduct the initiation in its entirety, making sure all rituals proceed in appropriate order and in excellence.
- Closing the space. When complete, the Initiator will close the space (see below).

An Initiator may perform more duties than noted above, or less, depending upon what you desire to have performed at your initiation.

Compensation for the Initiator

Depending upon what you're requesting from the Initiator, you may decide to offer compensation. Or, the Initiator may request compensation. What that would look like completely depends upon the 2 of you and the agreement you make. Put the agreement in writing so that it's clear.

There are a few underlying principles regarding compensation to keep in mind.

Money is not the first consideration for any magickal or spiritual undertaking. Yes, it is a factor, yet it is not primary.

In some spiritual traditions, it would cost you upwards of $10,000 or more to be initiated. In these traditions, initiation is a long process with many expenses, requiring intensive time and labor.

While I don't believe anyone will pay $10,000 or anywhere near that for initiation as a Christian Witch, we must give consideration to the time, energy and expertise you're asking of the Initiator. If the Initiator is a magickal master, with knowledge of these matters, it's likely they've been practicing magick for years and have invested heavily in their own spiritual unfoldment and in their magickal development. We honor this and compensate accordingly.

These matters are to be worked out between the initiate and the Initiator, keeping in mind that money is not the main consideration and the fact that no one can 'buy' an initiation.

You Are Sovereign

I feel inspired to re-emphasize an important aspect of procuring an Initiator. Never give your agency or authority over to another. There are no authority figures in your life save Higher Self, the real You. The Initiator is not someone whom you should be submitting to. The Initiator is a servant leader as we all are. Covens are in a circle because all are equal. No one is better than anyone else. Do not let inappropriate energies unconsciously slip into the process. If they do (we're human), become aware and clear them **immediately**.

Having an Initiator serve you in your initiation can be a powerfully self-loving decision.

Either way, trust yourself and you'll know exactly what to do.

Preparation for the Initiation

In this chapter, we'll go over how to prepare for the initiation, how to prepare the Initiatory Order of Rites, along with a step-by-step order of the rites and rituals involved in a Christian Witch's Initiation. In addition to the Initiatory Order of Rites, you may want to hold all the important details in a grimoire that has been acquired expressly for this purpose which we will refer to here as your Initiation Grimoire.

In the next chapter, we'll look at an example layout of the Initiatory Order of Rites as well as a sample.

To get in the appropriate frame of mind for what you're embarking upon here, reading Exodus chapter 26, Leviticus chapters 8-10 and 21, 1 Samuel 10:1 and any other Bible passages that speak of temple construction, consecration of sacred space and the priesthood could be extremely helpful. These passages can provide inspiration, insight and revelations, or just ideas we had not considered, which are all deeply helpful. After all, you're creating something new that does not yet have an established tradition or set protocols, as we've previously discussed. I find reading passages from the Bible to be extremely illuminating. The essence of what we are doing as Christian Witches may not have exact protocols, yet there are underlying principles, practices and procedures that have been used by holy people the world over for eons that we can call upon and press into service here.

A symbolic gesture could be to acquire a new Bible for your initiation. If you're in a coven, it could be a coven ritual to gift a beautiful new Bible at initiations. Just an idea.

Divination is always a good idea and can help with any and all aspects of the initiation. A pendulum swing can give definitive yes/no answers on certain aspects of the initiation, whereas a Tarot reading provides more comprehensive answers, with nuance, other considerations, people and a plethora of other factors we may not be consciously aware of (more on this below).

Please note: the following preparations do not have to be followed in any strict order. The reason I purposely refrained from laying out this information in a step-by-step, numbered and/or formulaic fashion is because we get to always keep this truth at the forefront of everything we do as Christian Witches: **Inner Knowing is the ultimate authority**. Always hold true to YOU and this initiation will be stunning.

Now let's turn our attention to preparations for your big day (or night)!

Initiatory Angel

Is there a specific angel who's been contacting you? Of course, we have a Holy Guardian Angel (Higher Self), as well as many other angels in our personal orbit. Some of these angels are task specific (they show up when we have a specific task to complete that they're charged by Source to help us with… this happened for me when the angel Damiel showed up in my kitchen at a time when I was completing the writing of a book and was having BIG challenges) while others are present to bring us specific messages. There are a myriad of other reasons an angel may show up in your world. The important idea here is to be aware and open.

There are angels of initiations as well. If you're drawn to a specific angel on your path as a Christian Witch, or a certain angel keeps popping up in your world (you see the name online, or you read the name in books, or this angel keeps appearing to you in some other synchronistic way), this could be the angel who will oversee your initiation. Ask. Ask. Ask. The answers will be given. There's no rush. Take as much time as you require.

If no specific angel readily comes forward as the natural choice, there's another approach. What's your intention? For example, an intention could be to deepen into love and banish fear as a Christian Witch, or to gain wisdom, understanding, insight and knowledge of the ancient mysteries, or to expand healing powers or psychic abilities. There are many ideas for what your intentions could be in your initiation. Select your top 3. Then use a resource that will help you determine the best angel(s) to call on for your initiation. I love this website for how comprehensively it covers angel correspondences: http://www.archangels-and-angels.com/

Angelic & Planetary Days & Hours

If you've elected to do this yourself (and are not using an Initiator), consult the astrological influences and the planetary influences to determine the most auspicious month, day, date and time for your initiation. Several factors can be considered here.

Now that you have an idea of who the angel overseeing the initiation will be, be sure to consult resources for the angel's day, hour and planet so that you can integrate these into the initiation, and for selecting the most auspicious month, day, date and time. You can use a grimoire for this, such as the Key of Solomon the King (*Clavicula Salomonis*). Dr. Joseph Peterson has one of the most comprehensive and exhaustive collections of esoteric works on the planet at Esoteric Archives. In the Key of Solomon the King, consult Table 1: Planetary hours, Table 2: Magical Names of the Hours and Angels, Table 3: Archangels, Angels, Metals, Days and Colors for each Planet. Then read Chapter 2: Of the Days, and Hours and of the Virtues of the Planets. This chapter gives a good understanding of the best times for particular activities.

After prayerfully and mindfully consulting these resources (and any other resources you may use as a witch) to determine the most auspicious day, date and time for your initiation, record these details in your Initiation Grimoire. The pertinent information will be later included in the official Initiatory Order of Rites.

Ruling Tarot Card

Because Tarot is a major teaching tool, and a mainstay in the magickal tradition, we cannot eliminate it from the path of the Christian Witch. As a matter of fact, Tarot is so central to what I do as a witch that it's only natural to integrate it into an initiation.

If you choose to integrate a Ruling Tarot Card in your initiation, there are many ways you could go about it, and you don't have to limit yourself to one card if you're called to implement more than one.

We'll look at 2 methods here. I'm sure with imagination you can come up with many ways to do this. Witches are ingenious people I've found, and quite resourceful.

The first method is to utilize one of your Tarot Birth Cards.

If you're going with this method, then select the most appropriate card. For me, that would be The Emperor (Key #4) for my initiation, rather than the Death card (Key #13). The Emperor serves me well as I consider him for my initiation, since he's about order, organization, rulership, discipline and a host of other energies that I'd love to pour all over this initiation.

Another method would be to do a reading. Either do a spread you're led to use to determine the appropriate card, or you could use this method:

- Select the most auspicious day, date and time to do this divination using the resources above.
- Separate out the Major Arcana for this divination (the first 22 cards of your traditional Tarot deck). You will not use the Minor Arcana. Initiation is a soul issue, and deserves a Tarot ruler from the Major Arcana.
- Cleanse and clear the sacred space where you will perform the divination.
- Light a white candle for clarity.
- Pray to ask Mother Father God and the Holy Christ Presence to guide and direct this divination for the perfect answers for you and your initiation onto your path as a Christian Witch.
- Invite your invisible helpers (angels, spirit guides, enlightened ancestors,

- animal totems, fairy kingdom, elf kingdom, or whatever elementals and/or spirit beings you work with).
- Fall into a meditative state, as you would before doing any divination work.
- Be still for 20 minutes or longer (this is the time it takes for your mind to be completely still, especially if this divination is being done at the end of the day).
- In a manner that's most authentic and soulful for you, spread the 22 Major Arcana cards in front of you, face down.
- Gaze at the back of the cards for a while with a soft gaze (as when you're reading auras). Breathe. Gaze. Breathe.
- A card will begin to glow brighter than the others, or your attention will be supernaturally drawn to a specific card.
- When you're guided, pick it up. (You could also shuffle the Major Arcana cards until the appropriate card falls out.)
- This is the Major Arcana card that will be the ruling card for your initiation.

A note in case you receive an 'untoward' card, such as the Death card, or The Tower card: fret not. These cards have powerful meanings that can be put to use in an initiation, and may even serve as powerful 'gatekeepers' to keep unwanted energies out.

Whatever card you receive, trust that it is indeed the perfect card.

Record the card in your Initiation Grimoire along with any impressions, insights, revelations you receive. You'll include the name of the card in the Initiatory Order of Rites.

Ruling Bible Character

For those of us Christian Witches who still love to read the Bible, or have fond memories of particular Bible characters, this element can be integrated into an initiation.

If this is not you, move on to the next section.

A Ruling Bible Character in the initiation is a person who:

- represents in physical form the attributes you desire to embody as a Christian Witch. For example, Job for patience, Solomon for wisdom, Paul for zeal, etc.
- you closely connect with or identify with.
- can be a guide and guardian on your path as a Christian Witch (more on this momentarily).
- can be an advocate in the Heavenly Council when you require a spokesperson in heaven.

Bible characters have always held a special place in my heart — whether it was Daniel in the lion's den, or Elijah ascending into heaven on a chariot of fire, or Jeremiah's unwillingness to step into his power because he felt he was too young — and have fed my soul and thus hold deep import for me.

This is may not be the case with every Christian Witch, so do what works for you.

If you decide to move forward with the selection of a Ruling Bible Character, consider: who will this person be to you throughout your life? If they're present for your initiation (Daniel and David and the Witch of Endor are all still very much alive to me, as is everyone in the Bible) what does that mean for you and for the relationship?

I view this as an opportunity to choose a sort of 'patron saint' or 'Orisha' for you as a Christian Witch. A patron saint is the saint of that person's (or that entity's) life, and all things pertaining thereto. An Orisha (in the Yoruba tradition) rules your head. It is literally your 'head spirit.' You know this entity well, and this entity knows you better than you know yourself. This entity furnishes you with guidance, wisdom, help, insight, revelations, assistance when you require it. You are in energetic and spiritual partnership with this entity, which will require specific spiritual protocols, including making offerings.

We've heard of witches or magicians or sorcerers who work closely with a particular deity or entity, such as Hekate or Isis or Diana.

I don't believe that this entity is the totality of Source. I believe this entity is an expression of God/Goddess that's personal to each of us. For me, everything and everyone is God.

You get to decide what you believe and practice. Make sure that whatever it is, it sustains you on the spiritual journey, and lights up and feeds your soul.

Let's look at an example. If I were to choose a Ruling Bible Character for my initiation, it would be one I closely relate to: Daniel. His unwavering dedication to his spiritual practices (even though different and even in the face of the threat of death), have always been a buoying energy for me. His unwillingness to change his diet in a strange land speaks volumes. He refused to eat anything other than fruits and vegetables, exactly as stated in Genesis as the original food — and the only 2 things we should be putting into our pie hole — the Creator provided for humans: seed-bearing plants and seed-bearing fruit trees. Not only was Daniel able to hold to this diet in a land of fatty and exorbitant eating, he was able to persuade those who worked for the king (in charge of fattening up Daniel and his companions) to let he and his companions eat only fruits and vegetables for a trial period and then compare them with those who ate the king's menu to see who fared better. Of course, we know who won that contest.

There are a host of other reasons why Daniel speaks to me. His 3rd eye was wide open. His dreams were prophetic. He was advanced to 2nd in the kingdom by 2 kings due to his spiritual gifts. He was wealthy. I could go on and on. You get the picture.

Daniel is almost like a patron saint to me.

Of course, Christ is the ruling presence in my life. If I was to pick a 2nd, it would be Daniel. I could also go with Ezekiel, or the prophet Elijah, both of whom I find both fascinating and endearing.

Now, you get to choose who that will be for you.

Consider:

- Who did you most love hearing stories about as a child?
- Who did you most want to emulate? (Some of us thought we were David

killing Goliath with a stone.)
- Who quickens your heart?
- Who feeds your soul?
- Who's story do you most connect with/identify with?
- Who overcame what seemed to be insurmountable odds?
- Who's the one that speaks to your spirit?

Not long ago, I asked the question on the Christian Witches Facebook Fan Page "Who's your favorite Bible character?" It was amazing to me how many of our witches mentioned Esther. Prior to that, I had not realized how prominent and influential Esther is in the psyche of witches. I think she was 2nd only to Mary Magdalene from the dozens of comments on that post. It makes sense. Esther was a powerful feminine (YIN) presence in a male dominated world. She was able to use all at her disposal, including brains AND beauty, to completely change the course of history. Kudos Esther!

Now it's your turn. It's time to go into meditation, or into your Bible (or both), to bring forward that amazing Bible character who can be a guide and guardian to you, during your initiation and far beyond.

Integrate the Elements

Integrate the elements of earth, air, fire, water and the 5th element ether (spirit) at every step of the way in creating, preparing for and performing your initiation.

Integrating the elements can be as simple as establishing an altar dedicated to the creation of your initiation and placing on it representatives of earth, air, fire and water. The earth element can be represented by crystals and stones. The air element can be represented by feathers and incense. The fire element can be represented by candles and/or a fire pit. The water element can be represented by a clear glass or vase of fresh, clear water from a natural water source (such as a river, lake or stream). If you cannot obtain any or all of the items you require, do what witches do and use your imagination!

Select the Location

It's important to know well in advance the location of the initiation so that thorough preparations can be made. Select the location by angelic communication, divination, inspiration or revelation. The space will call you. Make arrangements to secure the location. If it's at a temple, reserve the space for your date and time.

Because I'm a Witch who loves nature, and found that many Witches are likewise inclined (not all, I purposely refrain from making sweeping generalities, they're especially dangerous in witchcraft), you may enjoy an initiation in nature.

My favorite picks for an initiation location in nature would be a riverside, lakefront or beach (if you're a water witch), a mountain or on the rocks (if you're an earth witch), a desert area or fire side (if you're a fire witch), or an elevated plain or open meadow (if you're an air witch). There's a video on my YouTube channel that could be helpful titled "Are You a Fire, Earth, Air or Water Witch?"

In the Christian Witches Mystery School, our initiations are held at an undisclosed location near the Grand Canyon. You can imagine that this makes for a spectacular experience.

It could be a great idea to hold your initiation at a lodge or coven home where magick regularly takes place. This means the space is already 'charged' with magick.

Another resource which I find highly intriguing is 'Geo Astrology' (astrology by location), which gives the best location on the planet for you, based on your birth. This information could be useful in determining the best location on the planet to hold your initiation. Though one is not bound by this information, I would take it into consideration — along with all the other pertinent factors — and pray on it. The Geo Astrology resource is at Astro.com (enter your birth info and the results will appear on the screen).

Consider having stirring or gospel music for the initiation (or in meaningful spaces in the ritual). Keep in mind the musical components, instruments and acoustics when selecting the location.

Record all information in your Initiation Grimoire. Pertinent details only will be included later in the Initiatory Order of Rites.

Select the Participants

Determine who will be present before, during and/or after the initiation, and what each one's role will be. Will you ask someone near and dear to you to say a prayer? Will you ask your coven to be present? Will you ask witchy friends to bring food after a solitary initiation? When you've decided on these essentials, write them in your Initiation Grimoire to be later included when you type out, or hand write, your Initiatory Order of Rites.

Select the Initiatory Steps

This is where you select which steps will be included in your initiation, and in what order. Steps can include: prayer (feel free to use the prayers provided and/or referenced here, or write your own, or use Psalms that are perfect for the occasion), invocation of ancestors/angels/spirit guides, lighting of candles, stating your Declaration, completing your blood oath, and any other steps you desire to include. Keep it simple, yet powerful. Set all these down in writing in your Initiation Grimoire so the pertinent details can be added to the Initiatory Order of Rites.

Select Your Attire

It's important to wear the robes and/or magickal and sacred attire — from your undergarments to your headdress and footwear — that speak deeply to you and shift your consciousness into the appropriate space for initiation. Attire can include all white, or a selection of spiritually meaningful colors (we use this method in the Christian Witches Mystery School where the colors are black, red and purple), or you can wear your coven's colors. The intention is to align the color(s) of the attire you select with the entire occasion.

If you're been instructed by the initiatory angel of a particular color, acquire these robes, or go to the fabric store and make the robes/wraps yourself (which could provide greater flexibility of choice). You can be sure you'll have exactly what you desire if you make it.

Remember undergarments. Another possibility is no undergarments under your robes. Another possibility is sky clad (nude). If you're opting to go sky clad, be mindful of your location, the possibility of other people happening onto the space, and those who may be attending the initiation. If they're all good with nude, go for it. If not, consider what you'll do instead. You can still elect to be nude for your initiation (or certain parts of it) even if everyone is not okay with it by erecting some kind of tent or curtain between you and others (much like the 'holy' and the 'most holy' compartments of the tabernacle). This way, you can still have your nude experience, and you can also have complete privacy. The best of both worlds! (I'm an air sign, so I'm always going to opt for nude!)

In one of my initiations where I was nude with a group of people, there was instruction from those who were leading the ceremony for the men to turn their backs just before the point where I dropped my clothing. This could work as well. I don't want to be too technical here, so I'll just mention this as a consideration: there may be people attracted to you who are of the same sex. If you're good with that, great! I mention this because telling the opposite sex to turn their heads may not solve matters completely if the object of the exercise is people not getting all lit up when they see you naked. If that's not an issue at all, great!

There are 3 phases of garments to consider: what you will wear to the initiation (pre-initiatory garments), what you will wear during the initiation ceremony (possibly nothing), and what you will garb with or robe with immediately after being initiated.

For example, you may come to the initiation with all white attire: from undergarments to head wrap. Then, at the appropriate moment during the initiation, you may drop all garments for that portion of the ritual. When the ritual is complete, you will garb or robe yourself as a NEW initiated Christian Witch. You can choose all 3 phases of attire according to intuition and divination.

If you have an Initiator, be sure they know what you're wearing and when, as part of the ceremony may involve them presenting you with your new robes for you to dress yourself, or them robing you in your new attire. What could also be quite beautiful is the whole coven garbing you in your new robes. I love when shared community experiences elevate the occasion. Imagine, every time you wear that robe, you will think of and feel the loving energy of all your coven mates who were present for this beautiful ceremony. That makes for a powerful robe indeed!

Prepare the Reliquary

Gather the ingredients, magickal implements and items you'll use for initiation in advance and place them in a reliquary. A reliquary is a chest or box that holds sacred artifacts and/or magickal items (some reliquaries even hold the remains of dead saints because they were deemed supernatural in their essence or nature). The idea is to gather all your materials together in one tidy, neat place and have them ready for transport to the initiation site at the appropriate time.

Some of these items will require that you collect them in a certain way, or at a certain time, such as in a particular phase of the moon (this information is gathered by means of intuition and divination). For instance, you may be intuitively led to use the herb rosemary in your initiation, and have been instructed by your spirit team (all the lovely spirit beings that are around you all the time) to pick it fresh from your garden, or from a place where it grows wild, on a certain day and time.

Once again, there's no rush in preparing the ingredients that will be used in your consecration or initiation. Some rituals take months to prepare. A wedding may take over a year to prepare. This is no different.

Also gather the items you'll require, such as crystals, sacred symbols such as crosses or angels (that will be placed on the altar or in the space), candles, incense, ancestral items (the ancestors love to give guidance, so ASK and mind them well), pictures of loved ones who have crossed over to elicit their support from supernatural realms, your Initiation Grimoire with all your notes and instructions, your attire (robes and undergarments), athame, sword or dagger, altar cloths and any other items you use in your spiritual practice that you're led to incorporate.

These can be placed on your altar in your sacred space until the day or night of the initiation.

If an Initiator will be present, the Initiator is likely to also have items they will use in the ceremony on their own altar, or, if you're a member of a coven, on a coven altar.

Fasting & Detox

Becoming super-conscious of what we eat is a necessary step on the path of spiritual liberation and ascension. Sacred occasions give us the opportunity to consciously practice new eating (or fasting) habits.

The days leading up to your initiation present the perfect opportunity to fast. A Daniel Fast could be appropriate (Google it if not familiar, but it's basically fruits and vegetables), or any fast that works for you.

The most important aspect of fasting is that the body is taught to be subject to the spirit. There's a mastery to be revealed in willful denial of bodily urges. The body does not rule the roost. This is proven in the practice of fasting. The body is not to be suppressed, or judged as bad. It simply is not to be in charge. It's a wonderful servant and a poor master.

I see the body as a beautiful demonstration of spirit, and a vehicle or instrument my soul is using in this lifetime to ascend and to experience the rich pleasures of being human and spirit at the same time.

A detox or cleanse would be appropriate before your initiation, if you feel you require it. You know what your normal eating habits are. If you eat 'clean' you may not require a detox. On the other hand, if you don't normally eat well, a detox could be excellent.

Be sure to give close attention to and be completely mindful of your health in any fast or detox.

The Banquet of Initiation

If desired, you and all present at the initiation can enjoy a feast together after the ritual. Great occasions are always more fun if marked with a great feast! This is also a natural way to break your fast.

Consider the elements of the feast, as you would all the other elements. During what time of year will the initiation take place?

If fall, think apples, cobblers, cinnamon, cider, pumpkins, and all things fall.

If spring, think fresh baby greens, fruit, and all things spring.

If winter, think root vegetables, hot cocoa and all things winter.

If summer, think refreshing fruits, vegetables, lemonade and all things summer.

It's a great idea to ask for support with this, and even assign a person (or a small group of people, depending on how large the initiation event will be) to handle this for you. Make out the menu, then hand it off to those whom you trust, and are gifted in this arena, with complete confidence that the Banquet of Initiation will be amazing. The last thing you want on your plate (pardon the pun) is to lug food to the event. Delegating the feast to friends you trust is a beautiful, self-supportive move that keeps the focus on the sacred nature of this event for you and prevents you from being sucked into the minutiae of picking out napkins and picking up chicken. It can even be done 'pot-luck' style, so that everyone shares in the preparation.

Prepare the Space

On the day of the initiation, it's **critical** to arrive early to prepare the space. Take great care with this step, the same care you would take to prepare a church for a wedding or to prepare your sacred space for a magickal operation.

You will safely transport all items from your altar to the initiation site. Be careful. Wrap items well. Transport all sacred, magickal items in a safe, peaceful manner, concealed from the sight of the general public. If you have large magickal items, such as staffs, these may be wrapped so as to be out of plain sight of the general populace.

The first critical steps when you arrive at the site are to CLEANSE, CLEANSE, CLEANSE and CLEAR, CLEAR, CLEAR.

For me, cleanse and clear go hand in hand. It is of the utmost importance to CLEAN and PURIFY the space of all dirt, dust, debris, unnecessary items, and any and everything that is not required for the sacred ceremony.

After a thorough physical cleaning of the space (preferably with natural cleaners that are non-toxic), the next important step is to CLEAR all stagnant energy, negative energy, stuck energy, and energy in all the corners (energy 'cooties' love to hide out in corners; corners are also gateways to other dimensions) and ALL energy in this space that is not for the express purpose of initiating a brand new Christian Witch.

This can be accomplished by burning copious amounts of white sage or palo santo (sacred wood incense). Of course, be extra careful with flames, smoke and fire, especially in enclosed spaces. Another great idea is to use Florida Water, which can be placed in a spray bottle with essential oils for a very nice room refresher and energy cleanser.

Be thorough with the steps of CLEANSING and CLEARING. This cannot be overemphasized. We're talking energy here, so be scrupulous about ridding the space of ALL stagnant, stale, unwanted or disharmonious energies.

After CLEANSING and CLEARING comes CONSECRATION, a devotion of this space to the sacred task at hand: initiation.

Consecration

People, places and items can be consecrated. I've been consecrated and it's a beautiful thing. More on your consecration will be discussed in a later chapter.

Consecration is two-fold. First, it entails the act of intentionally declaring a thing/person to be holy, sacred and set aside for the purpose of God/Goddess/I Am, like a nun, or a priest, or a High Wizard. Next, it entails a new way that this item/person/place will be treated and placed into service: in accordance with all that is sacred and holy.

For me, consecration is as simple and pure as me committing to my divine destiny in a wholly new, intentionally clear and viscerally felt way. It's me being who I am and doing what I came here to do.

I trust you know well why you are choosing to be initiated (and also consecrated) as a Christian Witch, and that you have carefully, prayerfully and heartfully considered this step, and have come to your own deep internal **YES** with it. Anything less would be a fool's mission.

This is an ordination of sorts, though I hesitate to use this word because it brings up so much mental material (and possibly emotional material). We don't want to be too 'churchy' here. One of the reasons I left religion is because it felt like a spiritual straight jacket. Many of us may have left religion. Let's not make up another religion. For me, being a Christian Witch is a spiritual path, not a religion.

Please also do not confuse consecration with morality. For instance, in the church, it's a frequent misunderstanding that a consecrated person is not to have sexual desire. In the Catholic church, nuns marry Jesus and priests must swear off sex for life.

That's not what this is.

It's quite possible that some consecrated and initiated Christian Witches may be inducted into the Tantric Arts and thus have more sex after consecration than before.

Consecration is deeply personal for a Christian Witch and doesn't carry any of the connotations that exist in other faith walks. We're not better than other faith walks. We're simply different, just as Catholics are not better than Hindus. They are, however, different. We delight in differences because differences reflect the infinitely faceted nature of Source. We're all flowers in the Goddess' garden the way I see it. A rose isn't fighting with a petunia.

Only you know what your consecration to Source and the sacred work of your divine destiny will mean for you.

As for consecrating the space on the day of initiation, pray, pray, pray. I've used the 23rd Psalm quite effectively to anchor the presence of Spirit at many a sacred and/or magickal ritual and it works beautifully, sort of like a universal solution. You may find other Psalms or prayers work as well. You choose.

Why prayer? For several reasons. We'll talk 2 of the many reasons right now: **energy** and **sound**.

You're shifting the vibration in the space with prayer. Prayer is energy. Since everything is energy, when you pray, you are literally changing the energetic makeup and fiber of that which you are praying over or for.

Pray up the space. Carefully select and call in spiritual allies, prayer warriors and coven mates to pray up the space. Pray. Pray. Pray.

The second reason is sound. Pray out loud. Not shouting. Simply audible. Each person can be wrapped up in their own energetic swaddle of prayer, walking about the space at will, praying their own prayers. This is beautiful. I've experienced this frequently in spiritual community and it's so divinely delicious that I can scarcely describe it to you in words. You may have experienced this as well and know the feeling.

After you're certain the space is consecrated (this will be an intuitive knowing), move on to the next step.

Invocation of the Archangels

Calling in the mighty archangels of the 4 directions is a great idea, if desired:

- Archangel Uriel in the North, Keeper of the element of EARTH
- Archangel Raphael in the East, Keeper of the element of AIR
- Archangel Michael in the South, Keeper of the element of FIRE
- Archangel Gabriel in the West, Keeper of the element of WATER

There's a great written invocation here by Richard Webster (one of my fave magickal authors over the years). You may desire to use it as is (it's Wiccan based), or use it as inspiration to create your own invocation of the 4 great Archangels of Christianity, Islam, Kabbalah and Judaism.

Construction of the Altar

I love this step because I love altars! As with all aspects of this most sacred occasion, allow your intuition to guide you. Rely heavily on your spirit team, who will be speaking to you throughout the process. How do you think you came upon this information now? Whatever powers that be that are responsible for putting this information in your hands can be utterly trusted.

Use a sturdy, 4-legged table or a flat surface, like a slab of rock jutting out from a ledge (if you're in a cave or on a mountain), or a rock or boulder surface (if you're in an open meadow or in a forest), or the ground (works well if you're in nature). I wouldn't go the route of using the floor if the initiation is held inside of a building. Conversely, if the initiation is held in a natural environment, such as in a cave, I would use the ground to connect with the Earth Mother.

The most important thing to know is that the optimal altar space will reveal itself to you. It's quite magickal when we trust the process. This is easy for us. We're witches. We can't turn magick off like a spigot. It's who we are. It's in our blood.

Bring forward your altar cloths and pray over them. Pray at each step of preparation. I don't think there's such a thing as too much prayer (as long as we're not talking fanatical).

The altar has been thoroughly cleansed and cleared in previous steps. Now you'll adorn the surface of the altar with your chosen altar cloths. Take great care with colors. They can (but don't have to) align with the planetary influences you're working with, or the color of the angel who is overseeing your initiation, or your coven colors. I like to layer altar cloths with colors that are meaningful for the spiritual work at hand. Nothing is random. All is in alignment with the sacred purpose.

Once the altar cloths are in place, begin constructing the altar according to your intuitive knowing with all the items you've bought for the sacred occasion of your soul leaping up to heaven. Remember to place representations of all elements on the altar: earth, air, fire, water and the 5th element ether (spirit).

You may be guided by your spirit team to construct more than one altar. For instance, you may have an ancestral altar as well as an initiation altar. Go with your intuition.

An exception here would be if you have an Initiator. In this case, the Initiator may be the one to set up the altar, if that's what you both mutually agreed to. This makes it easier to find all required items when called for in the ceremony, especially if the initiation is taking place in the semi-dark or in a space that is only lit with candles or at night. The Initiator is a person who is more advanced in the work and thus knows what to do. You will have had several communications with the Initiator all along so that everyone present will be apprised. Do all in your power to have order and excellence rule the occasion.

After all preparations have been made, including any that are not listed here, rest assured that the whole affair will proceed in the highest vibration according to divine perfection, harmony and beauty.

Now let's move on to another very important aspect of preparation for initiation: your new name.

Your New Sacred Name

Somewhere in this process, a new name may come to you, or it may not. It's not a requirement.

If a name does come to you, this name will be your magickal name conferred upon you at your initiation. Your name is your nature. A new name was often conferred upon individuals in the Bible who had a radical change in consciousness such that the old name no longer fit. I believe the same happens at initiation.

Rituals and rites of passage are key to the magickal path because they radically change consciousness. Besides all the pomp and circumstance, this is one reason I love ritual. The change is radical, significant, instant and permanent.

Your new name will reflect this change and will speak to your new nature. Once the new name is received, if you're led, create a sigil from the new name. This will become your sigil (or seal) that you'll place in your grimoire (and the Coven Grimoire if you join or form a coven… more on this later). There are many ways of crafting a sigil. If you conduct a search, a vast array of options will appear from YouTube and elsewhere. Follow the method that intuitively speaks to your soul.

If the name doesn't readily come to you, I wouldn't agonize over it. I've been through several initiations (and recently endured an initiation with a Shaman in the Andes mountains in Peru in a San Pedro ceremony) and at each initiation, if a new name was part of the process, it floated to me effortlessly. Thus far, of the 4 names I've received over the years, none of them were difficult to attain. At 2 of the initiations, my new name was received from the Initiator (and I didn't know what the name would be). In the other 2 instances, the name came directly from the divine into my consciousness.

The reason I share this is because there's no need to obsess over the name. It will come. It may even come in the moment of initiation. Trust. This is a beautiful, powerful, mysterious, magickal universe. It will all come together in ways that none of us can predict.

When the name comes, it will become apparent whether this is a public name or not. The first name I received, directly from the divine, was a name that became my new legal name.

The next name I received (also directly from the divine) was a magickal name that was never to be uttered publicly (for as long as I used it as a magickal name). I was able to utter it publicly later, when I no longer worked under that magickal name. It's almost like there was a graduation, and I somehow outgrew that magickal name, though it's still fond to me because I remember who I was when I wore that name.

Magick as a spiritual practice is dynamic such that things around you change frequently and radically as you change.

The next name I received I still use, and was quite ok to be known by others, as it's used in my spiritual community.

The next name I received is public (KAISI) conferred upon me by Mother Ayahuasca in a ceremony in Peru. This is not a magickal name per se (meaning that this name is not expressly for practicing magick). This name is an aspiration for me spiritually and for my work in the world. KAISI means one who plants seed in others and nurtures these seeds to grow. It also entails my work as a healer who integrates plant medicine. Intentionally planting seeds of love, joy, beauty, bliss, abundance and more divine qualities in people around me is beyond my personal magickal practice. It speaks to my work in the world. Frankly, I feel this name viscerally and know it is a WORD symbol of the divine ideal, the true Self as manifested in this incarnation for this phase of my journey.

Your Consecration

1 Samuel chapter 16 tells the story of Samuel being sent by God to anoint David as the next king. Without going deep into the politics of the event, we're giving particular attention to the words in verse 5, where Samuel approaches the town of Jesse and, once it's established he comes in peace, gives the people there a directive to 'consecrate yourselves' in order to accompany him to a sacrifice.

Consecrate yourself.

Or:

Sanctify yourself.

Or:

Hallow yourself.

All these are terms used to describe the state of being in which one optimally enters a sacred space, on a sacred occasion, to engage in a sacred ceremony.

I cannot see how it would be any different for us as Christian Witches embarking on the sacred occasion of one's initiation.

Consecrate means to make holy, or set aside for a holy purpose, or to dedicate to God, or to make sacred, or all of the above.

A good exercise before you proceed is to pull out your Initiation Grimoire and write out — as completely and honestly as you are divinely able — what consecration means to you, especially as a Christian Witch.

I was consecrated long ago, and can tell you this: **it changes everything**.

It changed my self-concept, and as we know, we can rise no higher than our self-concept. It changed how I ate and who I associated with. It even changed my relationship with sexual partners, not so much because I was consciously seeking to change that part of my life. It happened energetically. The True Self would no longer abide me slinking around with people I knew I had no business slinking around with. I'd been too afraid to cut the cord. I feel like consecration, if undertaken appropriately, is a great b.s. cutter. It cuts the 3rd dimensional b.s. we let ourselves get tied up in, even as we know we shouldn't be tied up in it.

Consecration is almost like an energetic force field. It's initiated and upheld in heaven, so the heavenly hosts are now engaged with you in a different way, knowing you belong to God/Goddess. You yourself openly stated so, and chose to give your fiat legs by holding a heart-full, soul-filled, sacred ceremony, heralding this new information to both the conscious and unconscious minds of yourself and all in your periphery. Suffice it to say, your life will never be the same.

As you can see, this is not to be undertaken lightly. It's my sense that anyone who undertakes sacred ceremony in a frivolous fashion experiences the untoward results of insolence in the presence of divinity. There's a reverence that must be cultivated if not already present.

Reverence.

The definition of reverence is to deeply respect or honor. We hold clergy people in reverence automatically, as a result of our conditioning. I was in Peru not long ago after leading an Ayahuasca retreat and saw a priest at the airport. He entered the space wearing long black robes and a large cross around his neck. Instantly, before I could think, I nodded and smiled. He made the same gesture to me in return. There's an instant, unconscious reverence when we see a nun, monk, priest, or any person who's consecrated and openly lives this consecration. Why? Because of the energy of namaste: the God in me sees, acknowledges and honors the God in you. One who's consecrated is simply wearing the fact that they gave themselves to God/Goddess, the True Self.

When I use the words 'wearing the fact' I do not mean to imply that they are being arrogant, or prideful, or feel the need to make it known that they belong to God.

I mean they are 'wearing' it in their spirit, in their way of being. It's become the fabric of who they are. That's namaste.

We can see it, not *only* because they are wearing holy garb (mind you, many consecrated people do not wear holy garb), but because it has become their **energetic holy attire**. It's in the bearing, the presence, the smile, the hug, the regard.

You couldn't miss the Dalai Lama, even if he wasn't wearing robes.

These souls have become holy, living instruments of Source.

How beautiful is that? There's not a thing in heaven or earth that's better, and I'm not just saying that because I'm a consecrated, ordained minister and initiated witch.

There's another aspect of consecration to consider here: whatever is touched by what is holy, itself becomes holy. (See Exodus 30:2) I formerly labored under an untruth: that if I was holy, and something unholy touched me, I became unholy. It's actually the other way around. If a holy vessel is touched by something unholy, the unholiness leaves. Holy vessels literally become cleansing chalices themselves.

If you decide to move forward with consecration, let's talk about what that could look like.

Consecration Steps

Your consecration will happen BEFORE the initiation so that you enter the initiation hallowed. You can hold your consecration the day before your initiation, or the morning of your initiation (if your initiation is at night).

The most important element of your consecration, as with your entire initiation, is your **INTENT**. Do not be unnecessarily side-tracked if you cannot put your hands on a particular item. All will be well without it if it doesn't float to you. This is not about strain. This is about allowing.

Here are ideas of steps you could take to consecrate yourself (if you're in a coven, your coven may have consecration procedures and/or protocols), or feel free to use these as inspiration to create your own consecration steps.

Prayer

As with every aspect of your initiation, prayer is vital! Pray before, during and after your bath. Pray over your herbs. Pray over the water. Pray over the anointing oil.

If you don't have the prayers, or they don't come readily, turn to the book of Psalms.

Here are a few tried and true Psalms:

- Psalm 23
- Psalm 27
- Psalm 91
- Psalm 150

A good book to acquire is **Secrets of the Psalms** by Godfrey A. Selig. It provides exactly which Psalms to use in specific situations, and is a powerful resource for any Christian Witch.

Call in Your Spirit Team

It's important that you discover, acknowledge, lean on and lean in to your spirit team: your enlightened ancestors, spirit guides, angels, archangels, animal totems, ascended masters and any and all spirit beings that attend you. It's time to call them all in for their guidance, help and support.

If you're already in deep contact with your spirit team, this will be easy.

If you're not in deep contact with your spirit team, there's one way to get in touch with them that cannot fail: MEDITATION. Meditation, stillness, silence and asking will bring you inner peace, and contact with supernal realms. It will be easy to connect in any given moment if you've established a habit of connecting.

If you don't feel deeply connected to your spirit team, take your time and cultivate the connection through meditation. It could take years. It doesn't matter how long it takes to establish this deep connection. I only know it's worth it.

After consciously connecting with and calling upon your spirit team, proceed as led.

Sacred Herbal Bath

It goes without saying that cleansing the body is a huge part of consecration.

In Peru, as part of the purification before entering our first Ayahuasca ceremony, the Shaman purified us with rosemary and prayers. He literally beat us with a rosemary bush while praying! He beat all the negative energy off us before we entered to meet Mother Ayahuasca.

There are many ways to purify yourself. Some use egg shells. Some use rosemary. The list goes on. Here, we'll focus on using a sacred herbal bath as a beautiful way to cleanse the body, clear the mind and soar the spirit.

Before entering your sacred herbal bath, wash your body thoroughly in the shower.

Use herbs such as rosemary (LOVE the smell), bay leaves, rose petals (a personal FAVE), lavender (a witch can never have too much), sage, thyme, and even some of the mints can do nicely, such as peppermint or spearmint. Be careful of the mix to be sure the concoction you conjure is safe for you and your skin.

From personal experience, using the actual herbs rather than essential oils adds a much more robust experience, especially if you've grown or picked the herbs yourself (only picking the ones that give you permission, more on this in a moment). If all you have access to are essential oils, those will be fine.

Select a work space to prepare your sacred herbal bath concoction. This space should be clean and clear of any unrelated items, and have access to fresh clean water. The space should also be private, so you can pray over the herbs.

Next, the herbs. It's important to note here that the herbs have given you permission to be picked and used for this process. If an herb doesn't give you permission, move on to another herb. How do you get permission? Ask. Ask the plants if they would like to give themselves to become the energy that will lift your consecration. Ask. You will be answered.

If you've never talked to plants before, which would be hard to fathom if you're a witch, this is your golden opportunity to start!

Trust yourself. Don't ask too many questions about the process. This is not a logical or linear process. Just dive in and know you're one with all nature, so everything is communicating with you all the time anyway.

After you've gathered all the herbs you'll use, next on to beating the herbs.

'Beating' the herbs means we remove all the sticks and branches, add the herbs to water, and tear them with our hands until they break down to mush so that their essence is released. The water turns green and the aromas are heavenly. I like this option because the whole while you can pray over the herbs and infuse them with the magick that resides in the palms of your hands. When you're complete, herbs will be all over the place, which is a wonderful thing!

If you choose not to beat the herbs, you can boil them down instead. Throw them in a huge pot on the stove, like my grandma used to do, and cook them until they look perfect for your bath. Then let the concoction cool until it's the right temperature.

You could add lemon or orange rinds to the mix. These cut energy like nobody's business. Adding cinnamon sticks can warm up the concoction energetically. Get creative.

If you're in touch with a true Hoodoo root worker, they can provide you with excellent ritual bath recipes, and/or you may choose to buy the herbal bath already prepared (from a trusted apothecary). Many preparations are sold online, already mixed and ready to be added to water. The only issue with this option is that I prefer fresh herbs.

IMPORTANT NOTE: only procure herbs from trusted sources. Of course, you will pray over, cleanse, clear and consecrate any magickal items you receive. It's best to acquire these from a trusted source so that you know the herbs or items were not sitting in funky energy. It's enough to clean everything you receive energetically and physically without adding the extra work of having to clear funky energy.

Light candles for your sacred herbal bath. White candles are perfect. Use other colors as directed by Higher Self.

Be sure you have complete privacy for the entirety of your sacred herbal bath. You may be in the bath for a while. Tears may flow due to the deeply emotional and purgative nature of the sacred bath itself. This is to be expected and embraced.

Silence

I cannot overemphasize the importance of silence on sacred occasions. The mouth is busy. Closing it can be a blessing. If you can stay in silence from the beginning of the preparation for your consecration, all the way through to the time when you will speak in your initiation, **DO IT**.

Energy is expended every time we speak. If you can harness this energy, circulating it in your system for the all-important soul work at hand, all the better.

If you're not able to be silent until your initiation, be sure NOT to engage useless, frivolous or casual conversation. Keep yourself in the highest vibration.

Anointing Oil

When you emerge from your bath, you will want to have on hand an anointing oil to anoint your entire body.

A recipe for an anointing oil was given by God to humanity, along with instructions at Exodus 30:22-31 (reading the whole chapter, or the entire book of Exodus could prove useful for these proceedings... I've highlighted the ingredients in bold print):

"²² And Jehovah spoke to Moses, saying,

²³ And thou, take best spices—of **liquid myrrh** five hundred [shekels], and

of **sweet cinnamon** the half—two hundred and fifty, and of **sweet myrtle** two hundred and fifty,

²⁴ and of **cassia** five hundred, after the shekel of the sanctuary, and of **olive oil** a hin;

²⁵ and make of it an oil of holy ointment, a perfume of perfumery after the work of the perfumer: it shall be the holy anointing oil.

²⁶ And thou shalt anoint the tent of meeting with it, and the ark of the testimony,

²⁷ and the table and all its utensils, and the lamp-stand and its utensils, and the altar of incense,

²⁸ and the altar of burnt-offering and all its utensils, and the laver and its stand.

²⁹ And thou shalt hallow them, that they may be most holy: whatever toucheth them shall be holy.

³⁰ And Aaron and his sons thou shalt anoint, and shalt hallow them, that they may serve me as priests.

³¹ And thou shalt speak to the children of Israel, saying, A holy anointing oil shall this be unto me throughout your generations."

The anointing oil recipe from God is simple:

- 5 parts myrrh
- 2 1/2 parts sweet myrtle
- 2 1/2 parts sweet cinnamon
- 5 parts cassia (this is a hot one, so be careful)
- Mixed in olive oil

In the Hebrew Bible, anointing oil was originally used for priests and for sacred items that would be in the tabernacle. Later on, the anointing oil use was extended to include kings. At the outset of this chapter, we referred to Samuel being sent on a mission by God to anoint David as king. He found the runt of the litter (David) and anointed him with oil.

The kings of Israel were selected by God, and thus they became not only temporal rulers of the nation, but divine rulers as well. This god/man/king theme is played out throughout the ages, and in virtually all civilizations, especially in Egypt, where it was clearly understood by the general populace that the ruling monarch was a god.

The point is: both anointing oil and the sacred act of being anointed are important. And these weren't just important to the Israelites. At Esther 2:12 (KJV) we gain a glimpse at another use of anointing oil:

"And when every maiden's turn came to go in to king Ahasuerus after that she had been treated for twelve months, according to the manner of the women (for so were the days of their purification accomplished—six months with oil of myrrh, and six months with spices, and with things for the purifying of the women,..."

This is one tiny revelation of the importance of — and high regard for — anointing oil and purification treatments in the ancient world, including Persia and Babylon.

Making your own anointing oil and praying over it, for use when you emerge from your bath, and for use in anointing the items in your consecration and initiation (if so led), can be a powerful way to invoke ancient magickal energies and anchor them in the now.

White Attire

Though white attire is not required, it carries the connotation of holiness, or purity (which is what you're going for here).

When you emerge from your sacred bath, and have anointed yourself with oil, you can wrap yourself in white linen, if desired. If you don't have white linen, white sheets of high quality will do nicely.

Wrap yourself in these and go to bed, if you're performing your consecration the night before or the day before your initiation. If your consecration is the day of your initiation, stay in your white linens until it's time for the initiation ceremony.

Mind yourself well. Stay away from the general public. Remember, everything is ENERGY.

Crown Care

Be especially aware and careful of your crown in all things related to your consecration, initiation and your life and walk as a Christian Witch.

Your crown is all important. This is where heaven meets you.

When you emerge from your sacred herbal bath, be sure to anoint your crown FIRST. Then move on to the rest of your body.

When complete, wrap your crown in clean, fresh white linen. Keep your crown wrapped until the initiation.

These are ideas and inspirations. Use what works for you, or create your own. You are a witch after all!

Initiatory Order of Rites

Now that you've made all the preparations, and have recorded all important details in your Initiation Grimoire, you'll transfer the pertinent ritual information to a formal document called the Initiatory Order of Rites. It's not necessary that you call it this (remember, no rules, only ideas). You can call it anything that speaks to you.

As you write out the document, use magickal language. The style of language you use is designed to further cement in your consciousness that you are being inducted into the Magickal Arts & Sciences as a Christian Witch.

For the magickal quality of the document, be sure it looks old (just my preference). It can be written out in dragon's blood ink or any important ink you love and that speaks to you, and/or holds magickal potency for you. You can write it on parchment paper or any other potent paper you've purchased from a magick shop, or you can even make the paper yourself (look that up on Google).

Hand writing the document is preferable to typing it out. As we know, the act of writing is magickal. Use every opportunity you have (and can create) to infuse your magick into the process. If you prefer to type it out in a font that speaks to you, that works too.

Sample Outline of the Initiatory Order of Rites:

This is a blank outline that can serve as a guide and can be completed with the information and elements you've created, gathered and recorded in your Initiation Grimoire.

<u>**INITIATORY ORDER OF RITES**</u>
Day, Date, Time
Location
Pre-Initiation Name of Initiate
Name of Angel Overseeing the Initiation
Name of Initiator
Ruling Tarot Card
Ruling Bible Character
Opening Statement
Prayer
Invocation and welcome of our supernatural allies.
Welcome of our allies who are present to serve and support this auspicious occasion.
First Step
Next Step
Continue listing the steps…
New Name (if you desire to put it in writing here or you can leave an empty space for the conferring of the new name to be written in later)
Conclusion
Thanksgiving
Release & Farewell
Close the Circle or Sacred Space

Example of an Initiatory Order of Rites:

This example Initiatory Order of Rites is based on an initiation in a coven with the choice to have an Initiator present. In this example, the initiate has chosen to have the new name conferred upon them by the Initiator, which may be a coven leader. All of the elements can be re-worked, moved or adjusted to fit the initiate's choices. (Names used are fictional.)

INITIATORY ORDER OF RITES

On this the Lord's Day of Sunday, June 12 in the Year Two Thousand and Twenty
at High Noon
On the New Moon in Cancer
in the
Temple of the Order of the Daughters of Zelophehad Christian Witches
Coven of Salem
Comes
Ruby Esther Johnson
to be initiated as a
Practicing Christian Witch
with all the rights, privileges and responsibilities thereof
in the holy name of God the Father, God the Son and God the Holy Spirit,
Presided Over in Heavenly Realms by the Archangel Raziel
Initiatory Angel of These Holy Proceedings

Initiator for This Sacred Occasion:
Christian Witch Luna Bloodstone

Ruling Tarot Card for This Sacred Occasion:
Key #4 - The Emperor

Ruling Bible Character/Patron Saint for This Initiate & This Sacred

Occasion:
Daniel

Opening Statement Spoken by Initiator:
"We now open this holy and auspicious occasion, which has been decreed in heaven before the beginning of time and which now unfolds on earth, with this prayer:"

Prayer Spoken by All Present:
Source
we come boldly to the throne of grace for the blessing, evolution and enrichment of this soul, who is called upon the path of the Christian Witch. This soul is entrusted to thee, Lord.
This soul is guarded, led, guided, healed, supported, nurtured and supplied by thee, Lady.
This soul comes to this initiatory space, on this most holy of days, in these holy and prepared hours, for the purpose of exponentially expanding consciousness and fulfillment of the divine purpose for which this one is sent forth.

We pray for the Holy Christ Presence to guide all we think, feel, say and do here on this most sacred occasion.

We pray for the ministering angels to guard and guide us, lest not our foot strike a stone.

We pray for the enlightened ancestors to hear us and give us their wisdom.

We pray for the ascended masters to gather here above our holy heads to impart to us wisdom, strength, knowledge, insight and love regarding this initiate, this initiate's life, including health, wealth, relationships and divine purpose on this planet.

We pray for the animal totems of all present to gently guide us and remind us of our true divine identity and our oneness with all life.

We pray for all the nature spirits present to remind us that all is holy and sacred to our Great Mother Father God.

We pray for the elements of earth, air, fire and water to ground, bless, cleanse, purify and uplift our souls for the great work before us: initiation of this most holy soul for the work and calling of being a Christian Witch.

Our hearts are one.
Our will is true.
Our intention is pure.

As Christ declared, we declare as well:
I know you always hear me God.

Hallelujah
Amen
Ase

Initiatory Angel Invocation to be Spoken by the Initiate:
I now invoke the presence and power of the Holy Angel Raziel
The Initiatory Angel of these most sacred proceedings.

Great and Mighty Keeper of the Secrets of our God,
Holy Angel Raziel
COME
I bid thee welcome!

Great Angel of the wisdom and mysteries of our God,
Holy Angel Raziel!
I invoke thee!

As you taught Adam the wisdom and grace of God, and the secrets of manifestation on the earth plane, I bid thee grant me the secrets to manifesting the life divine here on earth, so that I may have the consciousness to fashion this incarnation into heaven on earth!

Holy Angel Raziel!
I invoke thee!
As you conferred your wisdom upon Noah, and gave the same all the dimensions of the ark, and all the secret knowledge pertaining thereto, I bid thee grant me secret knowledge of the mysteries of our God such that these may lift me into a rarified cloud of divine and sacred understanding of truth.

Holy Angel of God Raziel!
I invoke thee!
As you conferred your wisdom upon Enoch, and gave the same a glance into the holy worlds beyond this mundane existence, I bid thee grant me an even wider open third eye to behold the mysteries of our God beyond the physical plane and to convey these, as led by our Goddess, to those in want on the earth plane, who have lost hope in supernal realms.

THANK YOU HOLY ANGEL RAZIEL
for your presence and power at these most holy proceedings.

WELCOME.

Welcome of our Coven Mates and Honored Guests by Initiator:
All hail our powerful allies who are present to serve and support this auspicious occasion!

Attendees Respond:
All hail!

Initiator:

All hail to the Daughters of Zelophehad Christian Witches Coven of Salem!

Attendees Respond:
All hail!

Initiator:
All hail the Parents of the Initiate!
Mr. Samuel Leroy Johnson
&
Mrs. Mabel Gertrude Johnson

Attendees Respond:
All hail!

Initiator:
All hail the presence and power of the Ascended Masters, Archangels of the Presence, Enlightened Ancestors, Animal Totems, Spirit Guides and all other beneficent entities which have gathered for this most auspicious occasion to perfect, uplift and ascend!

Attendees Respond:
All hail!

Lighting of the Elemental Candles by Coven Mate & Christian Witch Gloria Raintrue:

As I light this red candle representing FIRE, the spirit of this initiate is fully fired and energized with passion and zeal for life, love and destiny!

As I light this blue candle representing WATER, the emotions of this initiate are purified and flow freely in a vast river of love.

As I light this green candle representing EARTH, the body, home and all 3rd dimensional possessions of this soul are solidified in divine abundance and fully grounded in FAITH and TRUST.

As I light this yellow candle representing AIR, the mind, intellect, communication and intelligence of this initiate are now harmoniously aligned with truth, wisdom, knowledge and justice forever more!

Amen

Attendees Respond:
Amen

Presentation of the Initiate by Initiator:
Now comes before us the initiate known as
Ruby Esther Johnson
to be presented before all onlookers here and before the heavenly court where such initiation has already taken place in harmony with the words of
Matthew 18:18
"Verily I say unto you, Whatsoever ye shall bind on earth shall be bound in heaven: and whatsoever ye shall loose on earth shall be loosed in heaven." We now bind on earth this initiate to God/Goddess/I AM, to the holy walk and way of Love, and to the soul's True Nature now expressed in all joy and fulfillment as DIVINE DESTINY.
Please step forward initiate Ruby Esther Johnson!

Initiate Steps Forward and Proclaims:
I AM HERE!

Question of the Initiate by Initiator:
Initiate Ruby Esther Johnson,
do you solemnly swear and bind yourself by your own blood oath to walk your path TRUE as a Christian Witch as only you can, to turn within for your highest, absolute and most intimate guidance and follow this precisely and immediately, to honor your coven mates and encourage, inspire and

uplift the same, to do all in your power to uplift and promote the magickal community at large, to fulfill your calling on this precious planet, and to live a life that is worthy of the calling of Christian Witch?

Initiate Proclaims:
I DO!

Presentation of the Declaration by Coven Mate Christian Witch John Lovelight:
Initiate Ruby Esther Johnson,
you have written a Declaration of your calling and path as a Christian Witch. Behold the sacred scroll and the dagger by which you will draw your own blood, taking a blood oath to do all in your divine power to fulfill that which you have written in your Declaration.
(Brings forward a tray containing the Declaration and the Dagger, without touching either.)
Are you ready to proceed?

Initiate Proclaims:
I AM!

Presentation of the Dagger by Coven Mate John Lovelight:
By this holy blade may thee be purified!
(Holds the tray with the dagger and Declaration before the Initiate.)

Initiate:
Lifts the dagger and the Declaration from the tray.

Declaration Read Aloud by the Initiate:
I, Ruby Esther Johnson, do hereby declare and solemnly swear that I am called to be a Christian Witch.

I answer this call of my soul with all I have and all I am.

From the core of my being, and with every ounce of my breath I say YES!

I take this vow wholeheartedly, without coercion from any outside force. This decision and resulting declaration is fully and unequivocally my own.

I DECLARE I will study to show myself approved.
I DECLARE I will regard my soul first.
I DECLARE I will love and stand on inner knowing first and foremost, beyond any outside influences, no matter how close to me these may be.

I DECLARE I will use the WORD of GOD aright.
I DECLARE I will walk in the LIGHT, guided by the Luminosity of God/Goddess/I AM.

I DECLARE I practice magick with complete alignment with the divine will.
I DECLARE I uphold, live by, deeply regard and honor the Witch's Code: to know, to will, to dare, to keep silent.

I DECLARE I uphold, love, support and root for all those in the magickal community.
I DECLARE I aspire to be a light to my coven mates, and an inspiration to all.
When they see me, they see Source.
Where ever I go, and whatever I may be doing, I vow to bring peace and never dissension.

I DECLARE I uphold and live by the laws of the ancient Hermetic tradition.
I DECLARE I regard magick as the Great Work and I take on this Alchemy of the Soul wholeheartedly.

I DECLARE all is well with my soul, and all will always be well with my soul.
I DECLARE I am a healer. I choose to use these healing powers for the fulfillment of divine perfection for all, including humans, animals, nature

and beings who are not in flesh.

I DECLARE I am a teacher who gladly shares TRUTH.
I DECLARE I am a WISDOM KEEPER who gladly shares my experiences as inspired.

I DECLARE nothing I see is bigger than me.
I DECLARE I am first and foremost committed to the Higher Self, my Holy Guardian Angel, the Light of my Soul and the Keeper of my Life. This Eternal Flame that is God/Goddess as me is the ONLY AND FINAL AUTHORITY in my world.

I DECLARE the WORD is a lamp unto my feet and a light unto my path.
I DECLARE I am protected, guarded, guided, richly provided for, watched over, doted upon, adored, cheered on and made whole, perfect and rich in every way by this delicious universe of life!

I DECLARE I AM A CHRISTIAN WITCH AND NOW UNDERTAKE TO DO ALL IN MY POWER TO UPLIFT THIS PATH WITH LOVE, GRACE, TRUTH, POWER AND DIVINE BEAUTY!
I DECLARE CHRIST IS MY HIGHEST IDEAL!
I DECLARE I AM ONE WITH THE ONE!

HALLELUJAH
AMEN
ASE

Attendees Respond:
AMEN

Blood Oath by Initiate:
I now draw this blood, placing a seal on this Declaration of truth, binding my word and my life to the life of God.

Amen.
(Initiate draws just enough blood to place a seal on the Declaration in front of all to witness.)

Presentation of the Completed Blood Oath Declaration by the Initiate:

I now hold this Declaration with a sworn blood oath high for all to see! It is accomplished!

Attendees Respond:

It is accomplished!

Conferring of the New Name by Initiator:

Initiate, having endured all the trials of initiation and proven worthy, having made all proper preparations in heaven and upon earth, having invoked the angels, ancestors, spirit guides, ascended masters and animal totems for their grace, presence and power, and having followed all the divine instructions set forth in this one's heart and soul in preparation for this most auspicious occasion, are you ready to receive your new name in harmony and resonance with your new nature as of this day?

Initiate Proclaims:

I AM!

Initiator:

In harmony with your divine nature and evolutionary ascension, you shall be known henceforth as
FYRE LIGHTWEALTH!

Attendees:

Applause, Cheers and Great Celebration!

Initiate Who is Now an Initiated Christian Witch:

Initiatory Order of Rites

I AM FYRE LIGHTHEART!

Presentation of the New Initiated Christian Witch by Initiator:
It is my holy honor and privilege to present to you the newly initiated
Christian Witch,
Fyre Lightheart!

Initiated Christian Witch Stands Before Witnesses
to receive welcome, hugs, flowers and gifts.

Introduction of Closing Psalm by Initiator:
After welcoming and gifting, we give thanks for all that has occurred on this occasion.
We seal the beauty, bliss and grace of this sacred ritual for all time with praise and gratitude by reciting Psalm 150.

All Attendees:
"Praise Yah!
Praise God in his sanctuary!
Praise him in his heavens for his acts of power!
² Praise him for his mighty acts!
Praise him according to his excellent greatness!
³ Praise him with the sounding of the trumpet!
Praise him with harp and lyre!
⁴ Praise him with tambourine and dancing!
Praise him with stringed instruments and flute!
⁵ Praise him with loud cymbals!
Praise him with resounding cymbals!
⁶ Let everything that has breath praise Yah!
Praise Yah!" (KJV)

Release by Initiate:
To the Holy Angel Raziel and all the great spirits gathered for this most

auspicious event in heaven and upon earth, we now bid thee farewell with great and wondrous thanksgiving!
And now depart with the highest blessing of our most majestic Mother Father God!
You are blessed and highly favored for all time!
We bid thee farewell until we meet again!

All Attendees:
WE BID THEE FAREWELL!

Grace for the Banquet of Initiation by the Initiator:
And now, having completed this initiation in good order, binding on earth that which has been bound in heaven, we now ask thanksgiving for the feast we engage in with our magickal family, coven mates and dear assembled friends:

Prayer:
Thank you God!
Thank you Goddess!
We are thankful for the banquet we now enjoy, the farmers who planted the food, those who picked the food, those who carried the food to us, and those who prepared and served these delicacies. We give thanks for the seed, earth, wind, water and sun that nurtured this food into holy existence for our sustenance.
Hallelujah!
Amen

Creation of the Ancestral Plate by Initiate:
Initiate takes the Ancestral Plate and places upon it a serving from each dish, then places the ancestral plate on the altar.

Banquet of the Initiation
All present enjoy the feast.

Initiatory Order of Rites

The Ritual Is Complete

After the Initiation

After the initiation space has been cleaned and returned to its pre-initiation condition, the guests have departed, the coven mates have been hugged and bid farewell, it's time for you to settle in to your new life with Source.

Just as after the wedding there's a honeymoon, after the initiation, have a honeymoon with Higher Self. You just gave yourself to Source, in a beautiful ceremony, with those you love present, or in a solitary ceremony. This is a monumental shift in consciousness. Your life will never be the same. Do not go back to your regular life as if you just had a regular weekend.

Take time off (prepare for this in advance). Go somewhere for a day or two or ten. Where's the most beautiful, solitary place you can go? Perhaps with yourself or a partner or a member(s) of your coven? A beach? A cabin in the woods? A luxurious hotel suite? A yurt on the top of a mountain?

Whatever glorious space may prove to be your respite from the world for a few days, be sure to give yourself the time and opportunity to journal in your grimoire, play with your Tarot decks, eat really well, and generally reflect, sleep, meditate and be still. Give yourself this gift after such a high point, so that you can process and integrate the magnitude of what has occurred.

Annual Ritual of Remembrance

The Ritual of Remembrance is performed on the anniversary of your initiation. As an initiated Christian Witch, there are a myriad of reasons for performing this ritual:

- To remember and honor the sacred and holy occasion of your initiation.
- To re-commit to being a Christian Witch. We all get off track sometimes, and re-committing is a great way to stay on track.
- For meaningful fellowship with other Christian Witches. If you're in a coven, it's a wonderful occasion to get together with the coven mates.
- To demonstrate how fulfilling this path can be, which inspires others to step out boldly on their journey as well!

How to Perform the Ritual of Remembrance

Very similar to your initiation, your Ritual of Remembrance is of your own creation and design and is deeply personal to you and your unique flavor of being a Christian Witch. No two Christian Witches are alike, so no two Rituals of Remembrance will be exactly alike.

Note: if you're in a coven, it's likely that the entire coven may have collectively devised and agreed upon a Ritual of Remembrance protocol.

If you're not in a coven, you get to make it up! Here are elements that can be included:

- Cleansing and clearing of the space and all participants.
- Music/musical accompaniment.
- Candle lighting ceremony.
- Opening prayer.
- Calling in the spirit team.
- Acknowledgment and thanksgiving of another year as an initiated Christian Witch.
- A statement of the highlights of one's spiritual journey during this past year.
- An intention for the year ahead.
- Prayers from members of the coven for the year ahead.
- A statement from the Initiator (or coven mate) of appreciation and acknowledgment of your service to the coven and/or community during the year.
- A re-commitment and/or re-statement of your original Initiation Declaration.
- Gifts, or the presentation of a gift from the coven.
- A banquet with the coven, or a solitary meal.
- Any other elements you're led to include.

Your Ritual of Remembrance need not be an elaborate affair. All the rituals you perform are really about you and Source.

III

DOCUMENT

Here's where you get to document your path — should you choose to do so — in your own soulful, heart-led, spine-tingling way.

Codify

Now that you've created and sealed your Declaration, we move to documentation.

What does it mean to you to be a Christian Witch?

This is a unique, personal, introspective, dynamic journey that cannot be summed up in a cute quatrain. It's a deeply devotional, mind-shattering, magickal path of the soul's calling that deserves our deepest attention and highest regard. After all, if your soul chose to incarnate as a Witch, and you add Christian to it, you've got a big road ahead of you.

Because this path is a lot like cutting through the thicket with a machete, you'd be hard pressed to find much in the way of a code of ethics, or parameters, or a system of any kind.

Being a Christian Witch is ancient, and as far as I'm concerned, started with Christ, yet it's new in expression, and deserves attention to documentation.

It's helpful to have a code to live by as a Christian Witch. The good news is: **you get to create the code yourself.**

I suspect, if you're reading this, you may have freed yourself from institutional religion (even though many Christian Witches still enjoy church), and have a deep, abiding relationship with Christ, in one's own way (if you were or are Christian).

Though there as many ways to document the path as there are Christian Witches, there are emergent themes, as noted in the beginning of this book.

I've been reading and reflecting on the comments in the Christian Witches community for years especially the Christian Witches Facebook page, where I have the honor and pleasure of being an admin in service to this great movement that's far beyond any person or Facebook page or group.

Emergent themes include, but are not limited to:

1. **CHRIST - Relationship with and/or being able to deeply relate to or identify with Christ** (either as an actual person, as a mythological ideal, or as an aspiration as in Christ Consciousness). I guess you could say this is where the 'Christian' in Christian Witches comes from.

2. **THE TRINITY - I've heard from many Christian Witches that the Trinity is critical to their practice**. It's not in mine, likely because my early years were spent in the cult of Jehovah's Witnesses and they don't believe in the Trinity, so I never acquired an affinity. I acknowledge the fact that almost every savior the world has ever known was one third of a God/Goddess/Child Trinity, including in Egypt and the Zoroastrian faith. There's a fascinating book worth reading called ***The World's 16 Crucified Saviors*** that reveals themes with regard to the Trinity (it's free to read online in PDF format).

3. **MAGICK - Magickal gifts that begin to express themselves**, causing the bearer of said gifts to begin taking account of one's life, eventually coming to the conclusion that if the gifts are psychic abilities and/or divination or the like, they probably WON'T be welcomed or fostered at the neighborhood church. Even though one of the divine purposes of a spiritual space is to nurture spiritual gifts for its community members, you probably won't have your gifts of psychic or telepathic powers nurtured and developed at First Baptist Church of ___ (fill in the blank). Though they will nurture 'gifts of prophecy' and other gifts deemed Biblical, it would be in a definitively non-witchy framework.

4. **INTEGRATION** - The desire to peacefully integrate being magickal and loving Christ (not an easy integration, especially after the very thorough conditioning from Christianity many of us have experienced). Yet, ***integration can successfully occur, when we drop the conditioning***

and turn within to the great knowing. As a side note, history is now agreeing with what Christian Witches have always known intuitively: Christ was a sorcerer (that's a discussion for another day).

There are many more themes. The foregoing are a smattering of the most frequently recurring. Basically, what we're doing as Christian Witches is integrating love of Christ and love of the Craft.

There was a word Spirit whispered to me on more than a few occasions before I actually did it (call me slow). The word was '**CODIFY**.'

Codify means to arrange (laws or rules) into a systematic code, or arrange according to a plan or system. We're not about rules, yet we are about laws (universal law). For me, the charge to codify immediately felt like ORDER: to arrange a system for myself of spiritual practices, rituals, protocols and holy days.

Why is codifying (or documenting) so important for us as Christian Witches?

Every important thing is documented… from births to deaths to Bar and Bat Mitzvah's to Sweet 16's to weddings to deaths. All milestones carry heavy documentation. You're buying a house. Sign here, initial there. You and everyone in the room knows you're doing something big.

On a spiritual level, documentation sends a message to the unconscious to SIT UP AND PAY ATTENTION. Something important is happening.

Our soul calling should receive no less attention (though it certainly doesn't require the paperwork) than a transaction such as buying a house or starting a business.

The beauty of this kind of documentation is that it's actually FUN and ENJOYABLE to create (I cannot say the same for business forms). I deeply ENJOYED and ENGAGED the process of crafting my own Christian Witches Manifesto. It gave me the opportunity to turn within, comb my consciousness, reflect, meditate and write out the 10 Tenets that are most dear to me as a Christian Witch. It's my modus operandi.

I happened to publish my Manifesto (only because the work I do calls for it). Yet, most Christian Witches will likely never publish their Manifesto.

It will be a powerful, working private document that one holds dear and sacred.

If you haven't yet taken the opportunity to CODIFY your journey — or to DOCUMENT — I pray this serves as inspiration to do so, if for no other reason than to provide crystal clear clarity.

If you'd like help, my Christian Witches Manifesto is for that purpose. To create your Christian Witches Manifesto:

- Select an auspicious day, date and time using the resources provided here in an earlier chapter (or a series of days in case your manifesto isn't completed in one sitting).
- Obtain a brand new grimoire for the purpose of recording your Manifesto, or Creed (or whatever lovely name you'll give it). Bless and consecrate the grimoire.
- On the day selected, sit alone in stillness in your sacred space, or a natural setting.
- Pray. Pray. Pray.
- Call in your spirit team.
- Meditate for 20 minutes or longer. Chanting could work here too (I love chanting the names of God for entering altered states of consciousness).
- When ready, ask your Self what's most important to you as a Christian Witch.
- Listen. You may receive impressions, colors, visions, etc.
- When you're ready, begin to write the insights and inspirations streaming to your lower mind from Higher Self. Continue writing until you feel complete.
- Go deep. Keep asking. Listen. Write. Give yourself plenty of time.

You'll know when you're complete. There will be a finality to the experience, for the moment.

IV

DO

*Let's get to the business at hand: what we actually **do** as Christian Witches.*
Let's roll witches...

Magickal Implements

Now that we've covered the Decide, Declare and Document steps, we've arrived at the most important step of all, the one that pulls it all together: DO. You've actually got to DO something as a Christian Witch. That's what we're addressing now, starting with your magickal implements.

First I'd have to declare to you that every magickal implement I have **CAME TO ME**.

Yes, they all came. I didn't search for any of them. In most cases, I didn't know I needed them until they showed up. In other cases, when I did go searching for what I thought I needed, I found something else entirely.

From my magick wands (every wand I have) to my magick ring to almost every other sacred magickal implement or tool I have, they were all presented to me, often in quite strange and synchronistic ways.

While it's true you may use many magickal implements in your particular brand of Christian Witchcraft, an unflappable trust that all is being orchestrated by heaven will go much further to acquire the items you'll use than searching high and low in every magick store.

Trust.

Allow.

There's no hurry. This will take years. Let it. Remember, the magickal implements' timing of appearance in your world must coincide with your knowledge, skill and ability in using them, or even knowing what they're for. This is not to say that magickal implements only come to you when you're ready to use them. That hasn't been the case for me. What I've ascertained thus far is that they come at the **divinely perfect time**, and in **divinely perfect ways**. Only Source knows what it all means. TRUST.

Remember, all magickal implements must be cleared, cleansed and consecrated using the 4 elements. If appropriate and you feel so led, anoint them with oil.

With that said, here are a few of the magickal implements that may (or may not) make their way to you:

Bibles

This may be one of the rare books that categorizes the Bible as a magickal implement.

For me as a Christian Witch, the Bible intrigues me like no other book on the planet, and speaks deeply to my soul. While I love the Bible, I don't take it literally. For me, the Bible is metaphysical, allegorical, symbolic, mystical, magickal and more. There's so much to the Bible that as a Christian Witch, even if I studied it for a lifetime, I'd never be able harness all the power within its leaves.

I read the Bible with the Apocrypha (the books of the Bible that are not in the official Bible canon of 66 books), as well as the Gnostic Gospels (including the Gospel of Mary, the Gospel of Thomas and yes, the Gospel of Judas), and the Lost Books of the Bible. Basically, if it comes to me, I read it. I have many Bibles in my collection, so that I can read the words of any particular verse in different syntaxes. I find this helpful. Sometimes one word in the Bible will trigger a massive revelation.

The Bible is like all Holy Books, it has a power and energy that if acknowledged, discovered and used, could move mountains. Bibliomancy is a beautiful and powerful way to work with the magick of the Bible. Pray. State your intention. Hold the Bible to your 3rd eye until you feel led to open it. With eyes closed, place the forefinger of your non-dominant hand on the page. Read the words. It applies to you. If you're unsure of the meaning, I've found the **Metaphysical Bible Dictionary** by Charles Fillmore (of Unity) to be a huge blessing. It's a worthy addition to any Christian Witch's library. I wrote a book on **The Bible 11:11 Code**, which I discovered is an oracle in itself.

Tarot Decks

I've heard it said that the first deck must be given to you, though this wasn't so in my case.

If you're new to Tarot, I'd recommend starting with that wonderful deck many of us cut our divination teeth on: **Rider Waite Smith**. I love this deck, and still consult it often.

We begin with this deck to learn symbolism. The Tarot is a book of symbolism. In order to effectively perform magick and commune with spirit beings in different dimensions, you'll have to learn another language: **symbolism**.

Symbolism is a universal language. Other dimensions do not speak English, or any other human language.

Symbolism is the language used by upper realms to convey messages to you. This is where it gets interesting, because though symbolism is a universal language, what each symbol means is not universal. What a phoenix means to me is not the same as what it means to you.

This is why your spirit team continually works with you to create in your consciousness a personalized symbolism dictionary, not unlike a personalized dream dictionary. This is critical for divination and dream interpretation. Joseph and Daniel both enjoyed these rich spiritual gifts, and were able to hone these gifts to divine perfection by their spiritual practices. You may have discovered these spiritual gifts within yourself, and have determined that you're an oracle, or a psychic, or are in possession of other gifts that aid divination. Divination simply means 'to divine' (to seek answers from the divine).

Tarot enables and speeds this process, and can be used additionally for meditation, reflection, journal prompts, story telling, divination, contemplation and more. There is no limit to what Tarot can do once fully engaged.

When I was in the early stages of learning Tarot (over 15 years ago, and I'm still a Tarot infant), I remember by Tarot teacher recommended that we work with one card at a time, over the period of a week, even sleeping with said card under the pillow. Full immersion in one card at a time was priceless. It was like living with a Tarot mentor for a whole week. Now granted, I had bizarre dreams, but I call it par for the course and totally worth it!

Over the years, Tarot deck upon Tarot deck has made its way to me. Many have come so that I could pass them on to a Tarot beginner, or to another magickal friend. This is the way of Tarot. If the true owner of the deck is not likely to go into a magick shop and buy that deck, the deck will still make its way to the true owner by way of people who are already working with Tarot.

The best way to learn Tarot is to ENGAGE Tarot daily. Tarot books and Tarot teachers are amazing, of which I've had my share, yet none of these will be able to rival what you'll learn through a dedicated practice of experientially engaging Tarot, and carefully noting all results in your grimoire.

Magick Wands

Yes, I have several magick wands as a Christian Witch and use them for many purposes. Some of which include:

- focusing the energy when I'm casting a circle.
- focusing the energy when I'm doing a spell.
- harnessing energy for magickal or mundane purposes.
- contacting spirits (wands are conduits).

There are more magickal purposes to a wand than I can put in writing. Every wand I own, including my very first wand (which is a forgiven nail), **CAME TO ME BY SYNCHRONICITY.**

Crystals

I won't go too deep here because I'm pretty sure, if you're reading this book, you likely have a crystal collection that could rival any magick shop.

It seems to be a pattern that when we first begin the spiritual journey, countless crystals are a natural and early acquisition. Then they turn into an addiction, in a very good way!

Crystals are our friends, and carry very important information and exude powerful energies. This is not a treatise on crystals. This is a nod that your crystal collection addiction puts you squarely in league with witches all over the globe and throughout the ages. Study and work with your crystals daily.

The Magick Ring

It's attributed to Solomon the king the saying that 'without a magic ring, no magic could be wrought.'

I know this isn't true, because I've done, and witnessed, a whole lot of magickal things happening with no rings in sight, yet I understand why this statement was made. (Reading the **Testament of Solomon** will give due background on the ring and its origin.)

When my magick ring made it's way to me, it made a huge difference. Yes, you guessed it, the ring came to me, as a gift, before I knew I needed it. I certainly wasn't looking for it. When it was slipped on my finger for the first time, something otherworldly happened. It was as if a lightning bolt traveled up my spine. Of course, the ring fit perfectly. A giant YES reverberated in my spirit.

It's likely you know by now exactly what I'm about to say… your magic ring will come to you.

Books, Books and More Books

Since you're reading this, you understand the critical importance of STUDY.

Christian Witchcraft is a **craft** to be learned and mastered. How? By studying all manner of related subjects, such as alchemy, Kabbalah, astrology (western, eastern and Mayan), numerology, herbology, divination, sorcery, magick, witchcraft, the occult and all the metaphysical tomes you can get your magickal paws on.

A magickal library is a sanctuary for the soul. As with all implements in this chapter, the books CAME to me. One of the most shocking manifestations of this was when the book ***Enochian Vision Magic*** by Lon Milo Duquette (a teacher I love) came to me. The universe made sure I received that book. I spent the next several months (and years) being completely entranced by Enochian Magic and performing the Enochian calls, which moves energies I didn't know existed.

I don't know any master who doesn't have a vast library.

Study to show thyself approved.

Candles

This is a biggie in magick. From candle gazing, to candlelit rituals, to candle magick, candles play a pivotal and essential role in all forms of magick that I've seen.

Colors of candles, placement of candles, timing of the use of candles, who lights the candles, reading how candles burn and more are all elements of the craft.

As with all magickal implements, 2 guiding principles prevail: work with candles so that your learning is experiential, and TRUST that you are being guided as to candle magick and how to employ this potent power.

Tools

I have so many tools in my magick space, from cauldrons to chalices, from pendulums to decks, that I honestly cannot keep up with all the items I have. They're carefully stored in magick boxes (my reliquary) and it never ceases to amaze me that when I open a box I haven't examined in a long time, seeking some relic for some magickal purpose, I come across all manner of items that I did not consciously remember I had, yet when I laid eyes on it again, fond memories flooded my mind.

That's called having way too many tools! But seriously, the tools have been coming to me for a purpose, and I'm elated at still receiving more.

A good idea would be to keep your magickal tools and implements documented in a system, similar to a library system. I'll be undertaking this project myself.

Grimoires

When I first began my magickal journey, I had 2 grimoires. One was for recording my journey as a witch, including thoughts, feelings, revelations and my overall experience. The 2nd was for recording spells, formulas, prayers, incantations, rituals, full moon readings, correspondences and specific magickal information I thought would prove useful.

While there's no right or wrong way to keep a grimoire, I do know that documenting your journey is a huge part of what we as witches do.

What could be helpful is to have several grimoires: one for initiation, one for daily journaling, one for spells, prayers, rituals and one for Tarot readings. You can categorize them as desired. After years on this path, I have mountains of grimoires and journals that taken together, serve as a silent witness documenting my journey.

Apothecary

Ah, the all important apothecary! We witches love cooking up concoctions and making up mixtures, for all manner of applications, so it's important to have on hand a working apothecary.

While it may not be filled with every herb and essential oil and potion, it will be your working laboratory, so go for it!

Have on hand:

- **Essential Oils:** (a MUST) all the ones you're called to. I keep 60-70 at all times.
- **Carrier Oils for Application of Essential Oils:** olive oil, almond oil (a personal FAVE), grape seed oil, coconut oil, safflower oil, sunflower seed oil and more.
- **Herbs, Seeds & Roots:** grow them yourself in the window or garden or purchase them from reliable sources that grow and harvest in a sustainable fashion (we LOVE our Earth Mother). Keep plenty of white sage bundles and palo santo sacred wood incense around for clearing energy.
- **Teas:** can a witch ever have a large enough variety of tea?
- **Tinctures:** a friend of mine is gifted in this and makes the most amazing tinctures and sends them to us. If you don't have someone else in your life who's gifted to makes tinctures, maybe that person is you!
- **Highly Useful:** alcohol, witch hazel (GREAT for skin), peroxide (great for pouring on cuts to disinfect), Florida water (as many flavors as you can find… I found more Florida waters than I could shake a broomstick at in Peru, which is sort of the Shaman capital of the world, so it's not surprising).

Many other magickal tools, implements and items may come to you over the years to catalyze the ACTION required of a practicing Christian Witch. There's a term in magickal circles that applies to those who study magick, talk about magick, read about magick, but don't actually DO magick. They're called 'armchair magicians.' Don't be one.

Practicing Magick

*E*ach witch has a personal brand of magick. Practicing magick is better than reading 1,000 books on practicing magick. It's also infinitely harder to do. However, this is the 'DO' section of the book, where we TAKE ACTION, so let's dive in!

While there are countless forms of magick and countless magickal systems, such as Hoodoo, Vodun, Quimbanda, Santeria and Solomonic to name a few, only you can choose what's right for you. I warn against mixing traditions. Mixing traditions and being eclectic are 2 different things. The way I see it, mixing traditions is born of ignorance, and being eclectic is born of wisdom.

As you KNOW THYSELF, study and explore the Magickal Arts & Sciences, you'll naturally gravitate to the forms and systems of magick that align with you and your gifts. This exploration is essential. You will not understand magick until you ***practice magick***.

Here, magick as a spiritual practice is spelled with a 'k' at the end (Aleister Crowley style) to distinguish it from stage magic and for other reasons as well, including the numerology of the letters.

What is magick? That's a big question I tackle in my book ***Confessions of a Christian Witch***, yet I'll give the Aleister Crowley definition here: "Magick is the Science and Art of causing Change to occur in conformity with Will."

The word Will is capitalized because it's referencing the True Will, which both Aleister Crowley and myself consider to be the Divine Will, or one's true destiny. The Divine Will is not some imposed dictum of a big guy upstairs. It's what we really desire to do, on the level of the **TRUE SELF**. Hence, his teaching "do as thou Will shall be the whole of the Law" does not mean do any damn thing you feel like doing.

Much to the contrary, it takes a mage of tremendous self-mastery, restraint, discipline, responsibility, connection to Source and power in order to live out and practice one's True Will: divine destiny. We are doing no small thing when we practice magick.

Each act, magickal or mundane, is to forward one's *destiny*. This is why I practice magick, to understand myself, the cosmos and my destiny, and to align with the same. If you're a mage going in this direction, you'll see mundane acts as important, and will consciously use your every day 'normal' life to forward your destiny. Magick is happening even when we're not consciously aware. Everyone is — in some way — a magickal being, recognized or not.

Magick is malleable, and therefore can be used for all manner of purposes, including hexing people, places and things. My approach to magick is to use it as a spiritual practice to ASCEND. I don't care about hexing anyone else, because I understand the law. (**STUDY THE LAW** as laid out in the *Kybalion*.) The Law of Mentalism states that the universe is MENTAL, and the ONLY mind creating my life is mine. Other people do not have CREATIVE POWER or ABILITY in my life. That power has been reserved for me alone. While other people can influence me, no one can create anything in my life other than me. The same is true for all.

A mage knows this and thus is in no fear of anything anyone else may do. Everyone can do as they will, though I've heard of the tendency to try and micromanage the universe with magick. Good luck on that one. God consciousness is all we require.

That leaves the question: what kind of magick do Christian Witches practice? Once again, this is a personal choice in harmony with the Will. Here are a few considerations.

The Laws of Magick

Magick operates by law and is in no way random. Witchcraft is included in the Magickal Arts & Sciences because it is part art (your creativity) and part science (law). I love science, so I see magick as very similar to the scientific method. While there are variants on the scientific method depending upon the model used, there are constants as well. I'll offer 2 models here, both of which contain 6 steps:

1. Ask a question.
2. Do background research.
3. Construct a hypothesis.
4. Test the hypothesis with an experiment.
5. Analyze data and draw conclusions.
6. Report results.

Or:

1. Make an observation.
2. Ask a question.
3. Form a hypothesis, or testable explanation.
4. Make a prediction based on the hypothesis.
5. Test the prediction.
6. Iterate: use the results to make new hypotheses or predictions

Here's how the scientific method (using the 1st model listed above) can be applied to magick:

1. Ask a question: what is the highest and best ways and means for me and my family to experience greater wealth, abundance, riches and prosperity?
2. Do background research: look up the angels, planets, times and correspondences that apply to wealth, abundance, riches and prosperity.

3. Construct a hypothesis: if I invoke the Archangel Gadiel on the New Moon in Taurus to gather intelligence on wealth creation, and I act on this angelic guidance, I will start to experience greater prosperity during that moon cycle and continually increasing far beyond.
4. Test the hypothesis with an experiment: conduct the magickal operation.
5. Analyze data and draw conclusions: did the magickal operation work as expected? What can I change for even better results? What can I add? Detract?
6. Report results: carefully record all results in my grimoire. If appropriate, share with the coven.

I do not mean to oversimplify, nor do I intend to convey the idea that magick is purely science. The truth is, you've got to start somewhere, and there's no better place to start than with a model that's already been created.

Since this book is not about the laws of magick, I would recommend you read Donald Michael Kraig's exhaustive treatise on the subject: **Modern Magick: 12 Lessons in the High Magickal Arts** for a more comprehensive understanding.

At the risk of sounding like a broken record, the only way to become proficient in magick is to practice magick.

The Cosmos

The cosmos, in my paradigm, is multi-dimensional and infinite.

For purposes of magick, you can utilize a 3-tiered cosmos of infernal spirits (the underworld and demons), terrestrial spirits (house spirits, land spirits, country spirits, plant spirits, elementals such as gnomes, elves, fairies, undines, sylphs, sirens, mermaids/mermen/merpeople, the phoenix, dragons, etc.) and celestial spirits (angels, archangels, ascended masters, spirit guides and heavenly hosts). The cosmos is mapped out. If you desire to speak to a particular spirit, you can find its habitation on the map.

The Process

It's always better, especially if you're a beginner, to have a system (or protocol) for practicing magick, then perform it the same way each time, continually improving your system until mastery is achieved. Your system will evolve to have certain processes that you engage each time.

My process is as follows, in 2 parts: preparation and operation.

Preparation - Getting Ready

- Intention - what's your intention? This is your 'why.' Write it out.
- Outcome - what outcomes are you seeking? This is your 'what.' Write these out CLEARLY. I cannot tell you how many times magick has backfired. The clearer you are, the better. One of my fave magicians, Jason Miller, teaches Strategic Sorcery, and that you get to determine if the outcome is best achieved by magickal or mundane means. You don't toast bread with a flame thrower.
- What entities am I summoning? If performing an evocation or invocation, who are you summoning? Why?
- What Bible characters can be integrated for the intention and/or outcome?
- What month/day/date/time will this operation optimally take place? If you're using one of the old grimoires (which I love to study and learn from, though my magick is much simpler), or a spell book of some sort, then likely all these particulars will be clearly defined or at least alluded to. ***Do your research or use the resources provided earlier.***
- Write out the **entire operation**, including each step, and the words you will state. This will include any incantations that must be stated precisely.
- Gather and prepare the materials. This tiny 3-word sentence is more than a notion. Some magickal operations can take months to prepare due to what I call 'cosmic weather' (moon cycles, planets, constellations and more).

- Purify and prepare the sacred space (usually my magick room in my home). Cleanse the space thoroughly and clear energetically with sage, palo santo and/or Florida Water. Construct the altar with items pertinent to the operation. Remember to integrate the elements.
- Purify yourself with a sacred herbal bath as well as ritual purity (fasting, no sex, no drugs — honor your body's requirements fully if you take medications — no alcohol), if required. When we prepare for Ayahuasca ceremonies, also added to the 'no' list is caffeine and sugar. (Cleanse your body with a shower before you enter your sacred herbal bath.)
- Prepare your garments according to the nature of the operation. Clean white robes and undergarments, sky clad (nude) or appropriately colored robes, etc.
- Prepare your mind. Focus. Be in silence beforehand.

Operation - Practicing Magick

- Prayer.
- Meditation, sound (bells, music, Native American flute) and/or chanting to enter altered states of consciousness.
- Call in your spirit team.
- In the sacred space, be sure to check that all the items you require are placed appropriately, either in the space where the circle will be cast, or on the altar, or otherwise. (I can't tell you how many times I've left an item outside a cast circle. If you do that, you can create a door with your wand, open it, go fetch what you forgot, then re-enter the circle and close the door.)
- Cast a circle (if the magick you're doing requires it). For instance, I've cast a circle and lit up elemental candles for a mushrooms experience, even though it wasn't required. Intuitively, I desired that circle of protection and light around me since it was the first time I'd had this experience and knew I would be traveling in spirit realms. Some operations ABSOLUTELY REQUIRE A CIRCLE of protection and light. Others do not. STUDY and PREPARE.

- Perform your operation in TOTALITY and EXCELLENCE.
- Complete the operation.
- Write details in your grimoire of all that occurred.

Start Here

If you're a novice to magick, or a beginning Christian Witch, **KEEP IT SIMPLE**. Begin with a Tarot reading on the New Moon and Full Moon each month. To prepare:

- Place a green candle for earth in the north, while asking Archangel Uriel for healing, wisdom and guidance.
- Place a blue candle for water in the east, while asking Archangel Gabriel for love, an open heart and healed emotional body.
- Place a red candle in the south, while asking Archangel Michael for passionate fiery zeal for destiny.
- Place a yellow candle in the east for air, asking Archangel Raphael for intelligence, understanding and the ability to heal.
- After preparing, cast a circle with you, your Tarot deck, your grimoire and the 4 candles inside.
- Conduct your reading.
- Meditate on each card.
- Listen intently. The universe is speaking.
- When complete, write out in rich detail a simple drawing of each card, along with the meaning for you, and insights.

Note: the colors are not set in stone. Do as your intuition leads.

I performed this exact ritual for years. This gives a Christian Witch 24 magickal operations to perform each year. The results may astound you.

Invocation vs. Evocation

Invocation (such as the Isis Invocation in my book ***Confessions of a Christian Witch***) is calling forth the essence of the entity within self. Evocation is calling forth the entity in tangible form outside of self. Both require incantations, prayers, rituals and/or spells. This is an oversimplification, so please do STUDY.

Angel Magick

My FAVE. Angels are immense beings of tremendous power, yet extremely accessible. Even if you have the gift of angelic communication, it's natural for almost everyone to be able to commune with angels. One of my all time favorite authors on the subject is Migene Gonzalez-Wippler. Her book ***Kabbalah & Magic of Angels*** is a must-read.

For me, the core principle of Angel Magick is alignment with God consciousness. Angels are more concerned with fulfilling their specific role in the divine order than anything else. To the extent that your Will, intention, outcome, the preparations you've made and the particular angel involved are aligned, the better.

If you're led to delve into angel magick, practice only this for at least a year. For a Christian Witch who's led in the direction of angel magick, it could prove invaluable to study every angelic visitation in the Bible and record the findings in an angel grimoire.

I have very specific angel grimoires, with colors and styles to suit the angels. For instance, in my Archangel Micheal grimoire, I carefully record the angel's many titles, herbal, crystal and planetary correspondences and any other pertinent information I require to work with this angel. I've found that by honoring each of the archangels I work with in this way, they've become more accessible to me at all times.

Angels-and-Archangels.com is one of the most exhaustive resources for all matters pertaining to angels and correspondences.

Another resource I adore for angel magick is Stewart Pearce and his **Angels**

of Atlantis.

Summoning Demons

I've heard it said that magicians don't care whether they're dealing with an angel or a demon, they only care that they get the information or the result they're seeking. With that said, remove all judgments that angels are good and demons are bad. If you take a page from the Bible, angels can be killing machines and demons have taught humanity everything from art to metal working to cooking to all manner of human activity in which no one would ever suspect spirit influence. Read ***The Practice of Magical Evocation*** by Franz Bardon for a comprehensive list of infernal spirits (who can teach you just about anything).

For my specific brand of magick, I commune with angels and cast out demons (spirits that are harmful to the host). I've also seen demons expelled by means of plant medicine. You'll have to determine the nature of your relationship with entities in spirit realms, just as you've determined your relationship with people in your physical world.

What's most important in magick is not who you summon. The most important component is YOU. Included in the YOU mix is your entire consciousness, including your unconscious proclivities (which WILL be brought to the surface when interacting with supernatural forces... more on this coming up). Do not be tricked or deceived by malicious spirits. KNOW THYSELF and STUDY TO SHOW THYSELF APPROVED.

Terrestrial Spirits

It's my experience that everyone on planet earth is in touch with terrestrial spirits, but may not be entirely aware. All humans are spiritual beings speaking a language of energy. When we walk into a home, we can feel the spirit(s) that reside there, even if only unconsciously. We take a walk deep in nature and are ascertaining all manner of spirits, though we may not have a context for it.

Intentionally breathe deeper and move slower so as to become consciously aware of the spirit activity that's going on around you at all times. Be attuned to these subtle energies so that magick in these spheres becomes more effective.

Do Something

I had a mentor who loved to say "do something, even if it's stupid." This is my charge to you: DO SOMETHING. BUST A MOVE. PRACTICE MAGICK. Mess it up. Then do it again. Get better each time. Do that over and over for years and you'll become a master.

Emotional Toxicity & Magick

Having a toxic emotional body is by far one of the greatest pitfalls in magick. If we think of the emotional body as an important part of the internal plumbing system through which magick will flow, it's easy to see that if the plumbing is gunked up, the magick flowing through this system will contain gunk. This means magickal results will appear in your life that are muddy and/or toxic. Let's do our very best to avoid, or at the very least minimize, untoward outcomes.

How do we become toxic emotionally? From the experiences of life, especially the negative, abusive or frightening childhood experiences we did not have the capacity or tools to process. These experiences and the accompanying highly charged, negative emotions were literally 'frozen' in the emotional body as a negative energy pattern. These energy patterns remain stuck in the emotional body until there's a conscious choice — backed up by powerful spiritual practices — to remove and clear them completely.

As magicians, attaining and maintaining peak states of consciousness — defined as unconditional love, enthusiasm, peace, freedom, bliss and ecstasy — is our highest aspiration and most important endeavor. You will literally feel yourself 'buzzing' all over when you're in peak states.

The law states that the universe is **vibrational**. As we know, love is a high vibration experience, whereas fear is a low vibration experience. Where would you choose to live and practice magick from? That's an easy answer. A high vibration makes everything significantly better, including health, wealth, relationships and magick. All the low vibration, toxic emotions and states of consciousness **MUST GO**. Set your intention and follow through with daily practices that continually eliminate toxicity. Don't be a train wreck!

An important distinction to understand is the difference between toxic emotions and the unconscious shadow. Toxic emotions must go. The shadow is not likely to leave, yet we can put it to work! I decided that there won't be any tenants in my consciousness that are not completely on board with me and destiny.

You could think of the shadow as the darkness we all have inside. Dark is not bad, it's simply dark. We would not have light without dark. The idea is not to get rid of all darkness. The goal is to put that vast energy in use to create magick and a spectacular life. Just as one can use the light to create, so we can use the dark as well! When we clear the shadow of unresolved issues, vast creative power becomes available. (Study the work of Carl Jung for a deeper understanding of the vast power of the unconscious.) I believe this is one of the reason's Stephen King is one of the most spine-tingling story-tellers of our time. He's completely familiar with the shadow, and isn't afraid to write stories about it. That's how he's able to scare the bejesus out of us. We wouldn't be so easily frightened if we had examined our own shadow and come to peace with it. Below, I refer to the shadow as your golem. We all have one. Put this big dark creature to work for you!

This chapter will focus on how to effectively and elegantly clear emotional toxins for a pristine emotional body, as well as how to clear shadow energies so that they work FOR us and not AGAINST us. The goal is to become a clear conduit for powerful magick.

Your Golem

In Hebrew lore, a golem is a creature made of inanimate material — such as dirt — that can be bought to life. The golem is created for a purpose, shaped into a humanoid figure, and then animated by incantations, or prayers, or by Hebrew letters carved into its forehead, or inserted into its mouth. It's basically a creature of mud that has been bought to life with magick, much in the same way God created humans from clay.

There are legends in which the golem is helpful, like a hero or helper. In other legends, the golem turns destructive.

I use the golem as an analogy for the shadow — even though it's not an exact match — in that the shadow can either be FOR or AGAINST you. As long as you're unconscious, the shadow is basically ruining your life.

When you engage in shadow work, you are getting in touch with this giant (who could move mountains for you), to ensure it's going in the direction YOU CHOOSE.

What to Clear

What toxicity are we clearing from the emotional body? All toxic emotions and low vibration states of consciousness along with the resulting experiences they cause, such as:

- Fear, dread, resistance, stress, overwhelm, insecurities, anxiety, restlessness, panic, doubt, hesitation, procrastination, haste, impatience and any and all expressions and manifestations of fear.
- Unconscious guilt, including sexual guilt (which a lot of us carry).
- Frigidity, no sex drive.
- Lust, uncontrollable urgings and addictions in the body temple, being over-sexed and/or sexual addiction and addiction to porn.
- Unconscious shame, shrinking, hiding, invisibility, fear of being seen and/or playing small.
- Playing not to lose rather than playing to WIN.
- Unforgiveness, holding grudges and/or nursing grievances.
- Anger, rage, irritation, frustration, agitation.
- Jealousy, envy, covetousness.
- Hatred of ANY kind, intolerance, racism, sexism.
- Greed, over-eating, emotional eating, eating disorders.
- Worry, being vexed.

- Revenge or the need to get back at people or make them pay for what they did.
- Pride, arrogance and secret longing for power. (Pride and arrogance are masks for deep feelings of inadequacy.)
- Laziness, sloth, irresponsibility, lack of discipline, listlessness and/or no or low drive or aspiration.
- No life vision, rudderless, aimless.
- Self-sabotage.
- Victimhood and thinking something is out to 'get' you.
- Poverty consciousness, lack and limitation.
- Little thinking and small-mindedness.
- Control.
- Comparison and self-hatred.
- Depression, regret, sadness, unresolved or prolonged grief.
- Low or no self-worth and/or low self-regard, which leads to weak or unclear boundaries.
- Being jaded, cynical and/or unable to experience pleasure.
- Low productivity, performing far below potential.
- Gossip, bickering, pettiness and attempting to plant enmity between friends.
- 'Dropping the ball,' not following through, not completing and/or commitment issues.
- A sense or feeling of being misunderstood or not being heard.
- Waiting for the 'other shoe to fall' or living in a state of expectancy that something bad is going to happen. Doom and gloom.
- Being exacting, overly demanding of self and others. Beating up on self.
- Feeling unloved or unlovable.
- Any need for approval, permission and/or external validation.
- Blame.
- Complication and complexity.
- Judgment of self and others.
- Handing over one's power to authority figures.
- Attempting to rescue or save people.

- Discomfort or uneasiness when others express raw emotion.
- Avoiding issues that must be handled and/or ignoring issues without giving attention to and learning the lessons present.

I confess I have, or have had, all of these, and have no problem with acknowledging it publicly. These are states of consciousness and experiences we move through, NOT IDENTITY.

DIVINITY IS OUR IDENTITY.

Add to this list ANYTHING you experience that robs you of peace. Then, have a ZERO TOLERANCE policy and DECIDE that you will completely rid yourself of all that is not LOVE and the HIGHEST and BEST EXPRESSION of DIVINITY.

How to Clear the Emotional Body

Myriads of methods exist to clear emotional toxicity. Whatever method you are using, remember that the unconscious is non-local, meaning it lives in your body, not just in your head. The collective unconscious lives everywhere. In order to have real lasting change, you're going to have to practice modalities that take effect below the neck. Reading books are great, yet if the material is simply a mental exercise, it will not do the trick.

The following methods and modalities are effective because they are HOLISTIC, affecting the mind, body, breath, soul and spirit. I'll offer 8 that have worked WONDERS for me and continue to do so, along with a short and sweet description of each:

- **Breath work** - I became aware that my episodes of fear were accompanied by panting. I slowly learned to use the breath to come home to peace. There are many breath work techniques, including Conscious Connected Breathing (which cleared MAJOR toxicity out of my emotional body). Begin with 2 simple practices: breathe more deeply all the time, and take deep breaths whenever you're perturbed or become aware that peace has left the building.

- **Meditation** - right after breathing, the most effective way to clear consciousness, though it takes many years. Practice, practice, practice meditation. It's that important. A meditator's brain is different from those who do not meditate, which means that in addition to having powerful emotional, energetic and spiritual effects, meditation is actually transforming your biology. In meditation, we withdraw all focus from the exterior world and the 5 senses and focus all awareness within. When this repeatedly occurs, one meets the searing, blinding light of the True Self within. Continued exposure to the inner splendor of the True Self burns away the chaff of egoic structures and negative energies. For example, a daily meditative practice is like meeting Isis every morning. You couldn't possibly have that kind of interaction repeatedly and not be radically changed.
- **Emotional Freedom Technique** - otherwise known as 'tapping.' Tapping moves energy through the meridians and can be carefully scripted for specific issues. The tapping points are easy to locate and tapping can be done anywhere, at any time, which makes it a practical approach to energy clearing. One of my all-time fave teachers on tapping is Brad Yates. His YouTube channel is here.
- **Ho'oponopono** - I first learned of this ancient Hawaiian healing modality from Joe Vitale in his book ***Zero Limits***. It's a simple, yet potent energy clearing and healing modality containing 4 statements of love, forgiveness and gratitude that is astonishingly effective.
- **Shadow Work** - all magickal practitioners would do well to CONTINUALLY engage in shadow work. What's the shadow? A repository of all our unacknowledged mental and emotional debris, unhealed wounds, unaddressed negative patterns and generally everything dark, scary and shadowy. I call it the 'basement.' This is the deep well of the unconscious where corpses go to rot and putrefy. This is where all the hurt and pain that we refuse to address goes to hide out and cause havoc. The shadow is NOT bad. It's simply dark. Witches love darkness, so shadow work could be taken on as the foray into the darkness we'd love to have anyway. A resource I love for shadow work is Carolyn Elliott's ***Existential Kink***.

The exercises are priceless.
- **Yoga** - yoga means union. Any movement that unifies the body, breath, spirit, mind and soul could be considered yoga. My mom's yoga was knitting. My yoga is actually yoga. Your yoga could be dancing, or swimming. MOVEMENT shifts energy.
- **Plant Medicine** - Ayahuasca, Wachuma (San Pedro) and magic mushrooms have all played a supernatural role in shifting consciousness for me and retreat attendees we've been blessed to serve at our Ayahuasca Experience retreats in Peru. Of course, I recommend you honor the laws of the country you live in. If plant medicine is outlawed in your country, you may have to travel to a country where it's completely legal. Plant medicines can be intense, so be sure to practice this healing modality with experienced guides and in a safe environment. I cannot BEGIN to describe to you the profound healing experiences I've had with plants.
- **Dance**. Naked. With loud music you love.

The ONLY way any clearing method or healing modality will work for you is if you PRACTICE, PRACTICE, PRACTICE until you gain MASTERY of your consciousness. Then beautiful and magnificent magick will flow through you. You'll notice your life and everything you touch becoming more and more enchanted.

Desired States

The desired states of being, or peak states, or 'flow' states include these and more:

- Love (not the emotion) as the creative energy of the universe
- Enthusiasm
- Joy
- Peace
- Happiness
- Bliss

- Ecstasy
- Fulfillment
- Poise
- Confidence
- Certainty
- Abundance
- Wholeness
- The experience of living with an OPEN HEART.

A collection of the principles to live by in order to become the complete expression of divinity and fulfill one's TRUE WILL:

- Faith
- Trust
- Patience
- Discipline
- Responsibility
- Harmony
- Creativity
- Equanimity
- Integrity
- Wholeness
- Honesty
- Perseverance
- Grace
- Compassion
- Kindness
- Power
- Generosity
- Accountability
- Commitment
- Elegance
- Acceptance

- Authenticity
- Courage
- Gratitude
- Respect
- Order
- Truth
- Wisdom

The fruit of the Spirit in one's life, as stated at Galatians 5:22, 23 is:

- Love
- Joy
- Peace
- Patience/Forbearance
- Kindness
- Goodness/Benevolence
- Gentleness/Humility
- Self-control/Continence

The longer we engage our spiritual practices, the more our actual character and demeanor will change. There will be noticeable RESULTS in who we are and what we think, say and do.

Many rich blessings to you as you lighten your load and BECOME MAGICK.

29 Annual Rituals

I've heard the question asked by beginning Christian Witches about the celebration of the Sabbats (the holy days of Wiccans). The answer for me is no, for the simple reason that it doesn't resonate.

When I embarked on my magickal journey years ago, I devoured books on Wicca, since they were plentiful. Not only did I not find a book on Christian Witchcraft, I wouldn't have known to look for one. I associated Wicca with being a witch. It was an unconscious, and ignorant jump on my part. *Well, since I'm a witch, I guess this is the way to do it…* even though I didn't ***feel*** it. I liked it. I wasn't in love. There's nothing wrong with Wicca. It just wasn't for me.

Let's go further. I'm a black woman in America and have been in contact with Yoruba Priests and Priestesses, and Akan Priestesses (a spiritual path from Ghana). Growing up in New York put me squarely in touch with Santeria practitioners as well. While I was exposed to all these beautiful paths, and can deeply appreciate them, nothing in my spirit compelled me in any of these directions either.

On the contrary, when I first picked up a book on magick in the Bible, a lightning bolt shot through my whole being! When I first read about Solomon and his magickal antics with demons (whether they were actually performed by him or not), my whole soul lit on fire! When I first discovered the Kabbalah, I was, and remain, RIVETED.

By resonance, you will know what lights up your WHOLE SOUL. GO IN THAT DIRECTION and none other. If you haven't experienced 'soul-on-fire' yet, TRUST that it will happen. I didn't find what LIT UP MY WHOLE SELF ON COSMIC FIRE until I dug deep into magick and the occult.

This is the long and short of why the 8 Sabbats never spoke to me, and thus why I didn't take them on as spiritual practices.

What I'll offer here are the 29 opportunities to create your very own Christian Witches Celebration Year (28 of which are based on the lunar and solar cycles). These are not completely dissimilar to the Wiccan Wheel of the Year, so you may see correspondences.

Covens can come together once per month, or more often, if desired and agreed upon by all members. The 29 opportunities for celebration are:

- 12 New Moons
- 12 Full Moons
- The Winter Solstice
- The Spring Equinox
- The Summer Solstice
- The Fall Equinox
- Your Ritual of Remembrance (the anniversary of your initiation)

12 New Moons

On the New Moon we plant seeds of intention. We expect these to come to fruition over the moon cycle. We get to start projects, start new relationships, and generally INITIATE GOOD in our life, home, community and in the world. You can conduct a New Moon Tarot reading.

If you're in a coven, you can come together to plant seeds of intention for the New Moon. Or you can practice it as a solitary ritual. What new intentions are you setting? How will you record and/or illustrate these in your grimoire? How will you track the results?

12 Full Moons

On the Full Moon we get to RELEASE. I call it 'cosmic take out the trash day.' Everything you're done with can go. What are you complete with? What are you releasing? What must go?

The Full Moon is one of my favorite occasions to do a reading. I usually like to do an in-depth Tarot reading using the Celtic Cross spread, or any spread that will give rich detail, layer upon layer. If you're in a coven, a group reading under the Full Moon, outdoors if weather and circumstances permit, could be glorious. A solitary reading is equally glorious.

The Winter Solstice

Though winter is not my favorite time of year, I do love the winter solstice, the shortest day of the year, because it signals the sun's return. After the dark of winter, the days start to grow longer and longer. We know we will emerge from the darkness. Sunny and warm days are ahead. What can you and/or your coven do to celebrate the shortest day of the year?

The Spring Equinox

The day and night are completely equal on the spring equinox (also known as the vernal equinox), when the sun crosses the celestial equator heading north. What can you and/or your coven do to celebrate the equal day and night we experience on the spring equinox?

The Summer Solstice

We've arrived at the longest day of year on the summer solstice, and the herald of the coming darkness. Though it's still warm and sunny, the days from this point forward will become progressively shorter, until an equaling of night and day occurs on the Fall Equinox. What you can and/or your coven do to celebrate the longest day of the year, with the greatest sun energy available to us?

The Fall Equinox

The day and night have become exactly equal and balanced again, as if there's a standoff between light and dark. Which will win? As we know, the days are getting shorter and shorter, which means the dark is winning, for now. Because nature is intelligent, wise, balanced and harmonized, if we align our soul with these cosmic forces, we thrive. What can you and/or your coven do to honor and celebrate the equality of darkness and light?

Write your ideas and inspirations in your grimoire to formulate your own celebratory rituals throughout the month and year as a practicing Christian Witch.

Coven Formation

Being a member of a coven, or choosing to form one, is a pivotal decision, with profound spiritual, emotional, mental and physical ramifications. I would form a coven or join one ONLY if led by Source. I'd also perform divination for guidance on the particulars, as well as at each important step along the way.

Christian Witches who choose to form covens could grow exponentially from being in intimate community with like-minded magickal practitioners, especially because Christian Witchcraft does not have formal temples, lodges or shrines, as is the case with many other magickal traditions.

If you're a practicing Christian Witch, you may have experienced (as I did in the beginning) being outcast by both Christians and witches to some extent, with few resources to turn to, and not many others around who are on a likewise path.

Personally, I'd love to see a vast multitude of Christian Witches covens formed globally, for support, inspiration, spiritual community and camaraderie among witches who, although do not practice exactly alike (and don't have to) have a common bond: love of Christ and the Craft.

Here are a few considerations on coven creation if you desire to form one or join one:

Equanimity

For me, a coven is an equal democracy with no hierarchy. Inequalities breed co-dependence. In the process of coven formation, you will likely be led to practicing Christian Witches who stand toe to toe with you, who challenge you and love you and lift you and won't let you get away with crap.

I realize there are covens in other traditions that have a High Priest/Priestess for life. This person or couple will always be the head or leaders of the coven. I don't see it this way for a Christian Witches Coven I would form. Even though I'm a natural born leader who's often thrust into leadership positions, I enjoy the opportunities when I can sit down and let others lead.

You decide what works for you.

Law

One of the first considerations is **universal law**. The Law of Vibration says everything vibrates. The Law of Correspondence mandates that there's an inner correspondence to everything we perceive on the outside. These laws (as well as the totality of the 7 Hermetic Laws found in the ***Kybalion***) rule EVERYTHING. We cannot escape law.

With that said, you may be thinking of who you'll invite into the coven and may even write out attributes of the ideal Christian Witches to join you.

At the end of the day, the Law governs who shows up. So if members show up who get on your nerves, keep it LAWFUL and look in the mirror. Remember: there is no 'other.'

Size

Start off with 3 Christian Witches. If you're the one who's starting the coven, pray to meet up with the other 2 Christian Witches to start the coven. If Source led you to form the coven in the first place, It will also supernaturally connect you to the other members.

The 3 of you form a holy trinity. By correspondence, all 4 of the 3's in the

Minor Arcana of the book of Tarot are about partnership, team work and coming together in community. You can keep it at 3 members for as long as you like.

If you seek to grow beyond 3, eventually you can add in member by member, allowing each new member time and space to integrate into the coven. I wouldn't advise adding more than 1 member at a time. Work with the new member for at least 6 months to see if this is a good match, and to fully integrate the new member into the coven.

This process would be different if we were speaking of a book club. I've been in a book club for 20 years. There are 7 of us altogether, which makes for a beautiful and full symmetry of tastes, opinions, likes and dislikes. There's enough variety, yet not so much that it becomes unwieldy. Over the years, we've grown intimate and protect our intimate space. You'd be hard pressed to even get an invite to one of our book club meetings!

In magick, we're working with energies that are even more potent and intimate than in a book club. You'll want to do all in your power to get this right. A lot is riding on it.

If you choose to expand the coven, go for 5-7 members in total. Under 5 members may not provide the breadth and depth of variety of experience, and more than 7 members may open the door for the group to devolve into sub-factions, neither of which is desirable.

Of course, there are no hard and fast rules. These are guidelines. You may find large working covens of up to 10 to 12 members, and other covens who form a powerful holy trinity.

Since it could be a sticky situation to ask members to leave if they don't work out, it's best to keep it manageable in the beginning. When the coven's rituals and protocols are solidified through PRACTICE, it can grow. Better to start small and grow than to jump in at the deep end of the pool with a lot of people and experience havoc. As with all things magick, follow your Inner Knowing.

Birth Date of the Coven

Selecting the birth date of the coven is critically important. Just as the soul chooses its exact entry point into this 3rd dimensional reality, so too do we give care to the exact date the coven will be born.

If you've found the other 2 Christian Witches who will form the holy trinity in a coven with you, begin working together on the official birth date of the coven using the resources provided in the chapter in this book titled: ***Your Birth Code*** (in section 2).

Find the most appropriate birth date for the coven based on the ideals and principles you desire to anchor. What will the coven's Galactic Signature or sun sign be? You get to choose.

Pray. Pray. Pray. Divination. Divination. Divination.

Once you've determined the absolutely best day and date for the official birth of the coven, begin preparations for the ritual that will take place on this date, just as you would prepare for the due date of a baby.

Coven Opening Ritual

To mark the sacred day of the coven's formation, hold an opening ritual on the day that will serve as the coven's official anniversary (birthday) each year. The 3 of you can include in the ritual all the meaningful steps for this momentous day. These steps can be drawn from the initiation and consecration steps, with the exception that they will be done for the coven rather than for an individual. An annual observation of the coven's formation can be created into a ritual as well. Write out all steps in the Coven Grimoire (see below), and prepare for and conduct the Coven Opening Ritual.

Commitment

Commitment is of the highest importance. The divine act of forming or joining a coven is not an experiment or a passing fancy. Ask coven members to commit for at least a year, attending all coven functions during that time.

The ultimate goal is for the coven to be together for years, and to grow in community both spiritually and magickally. Let each member decide if they'd like to renew for the following year. You'll end up with the perfect blend of Christian Witches who'll be together for years, love it and create the most gorgeously gratifying memories.

Coven Agreement

To reflect the commitment each one is making to the coven, write out a simple coven agreement that members sign and agree to when joining. This is more for the purpose of establishing healthy boundaries for all and to provide each member with clarity on what is acceptable and what is not. These days, one cannot even join a Facebook Group without agreeing to the rules as set forth by the administrators of the group, because we understand how people can be.

Some may require reminders from time to time, which is to be expected. Yet, if there's a member who notoriously does not honor agreements, I don't see any reason not to invite them to leave. Remember, this is all voluntary. No one is beholden to anyone else.

Without being too lengthy or wordy, a coven agreement can contain these elements:

- Confidentiality - NEVER reveal the identity of coven mates. Make sure members agree to this stipulation, even if they should choose at some future point to leave the coven, for whatever reason.
- Logistics - meeting times, frequency and location and a YES from the member that they will do all in their power to make the meetings the highest priority. Grace is a yes. Irresponsibility is a no.
- Responsibilities - the responsibilities all coven members have agreed to, for instance, burning a candle on one's personal altar for the coven, bringing certain items to the meetings, etc.
- Respect and honor - a general guideline that all will respect and honor each other, and that if there are disagreements, how they will be resolved.

If you have mature people working together, and Source has sourced this coven, you won't have big blow-ups to concern yourself with. Any and all disagreements can be addressed and resolved with love and support.

- Arbitration - if you absolutely cannot reach an agreement, have an arbitration option. Arbitration in this case is distinct from the legal definition in that here you would have magickal elders, or witches you all respect, who have agreed to give their wise counsel if required. While the elders won't make a decision, they can offer wisdom born of experience that could benefit the coven in sorting its own disagreements and coming to harmonious outcomes that benefit all.
- Reminder of Law - make sure everyone in the coven agrees to keep it lawful, which means that everything everyone sees and/or experiences, is a function of one's own consciousness. This is a safe space for all to take personal responsibility with a zero-blame and zero-projection policy.

There may be more items you'd like members to agree to. Do not be too exacting. We're all starting out on a fairly new venture in which we'll learn and grow together as Christian Witches. Be flexible and willing to adjust the agreement if doing so is in the best interests of all coven members.

Better than a bunch of rules is a solid framework based on law and principle that brings forth and cultivates the very best character in each person.

Meeting Frequency

Decide on a meeting frequency that works for all coven members. Once per month on the new moon or full moon are ideal (or you can meet on both if all agree). Having 100% participation at all the meetings is ideal, though it's important to be understanding of circumstances when this may not be possible. However, observe if members are routinely not making meetings. It could signal that the meetings are not adding value, or it may be an opportunity for coven members to recommit. Deciding on meeting frequency along with dates and times will be easier with fewer people in the beginning. Record all coven meetings — and all witches present at each meeting — in the Coven Grimoire.

Location

Choose a location that is as equidistant to all coven members as you can. Keep it easy enough for each member to build meetings into their schedule, like going to church or the yoga studio. If coven members lives far from one other, you may choose to have quarterly meetings on the equinoxes and solstices and spend the day together.

If the location is in a person's home, **be sure the space in the home where the meetings are conducted is consecrated, private and ready for magick**. and not in the middle of someone's living room with kids running around and a television blaring. Have an attitude of reverence and ceremony that elevates your coven and puts you in immediate contact with subtle energies.

Online Covens

I do NOT recommend online covens, for many reasons. First and foremost, everything is energy. We cannot ascertain a person's energy field online in the same way we can in person. I realize we live in a highly advanced technological society. I embrace technology while holding true to my roots in spirituality. The personal presence of other beings — especially the beings with whom I'm choosing to be magickally intimate — is important to me. I am super careful about who I practice magick with, who I break bread with, and who I allow into my **intimate energetic space**. I would offer you do the same. Remember, energy bleeds, for better or for worse.

Coven Leadership

Rotate coven leadership so no one gets a big head. If we're not careful, heads can grow. The way to forestall this very human tendency is to install systems that cut arrogance, pride and better-than off at the knees and keep humility and servant leadership at the forefront of everyone's mind.

I would offer that if there's an initiated Christian Witch present, let this one be the first to lead the coven, if all agree. If everyone is initiated, cast a group divination to determine who fills each role. I'm not necessarily fond of casting votes for leadership as it could possibly introduce an air of politics into the coven, which could be disastrous.

For me, a properly cast divination answers every question unequivocally.

There may be resistance to allowing younger practicing Christian Witches to lead. I've found the best way to learn how to do anything is to do it, mess it up, then do it again until you've mastered it. There can be many roles in coven leadership, from the Coven High Witch/Wizard/Warlock to the 2nd in command (who leads in cases where the leader is not present) to those who are charged with altar construction, or caring for the coven's reliquary. If agreed upon by all members, coven leadership can rotate each year on the anniversary of the coven.

Coven Name/Bible Character

A Bible name can be used as a coven name. Reflect and meditate on the DIVINE ATTRIBUTES you desire to be the ENERGETIC FOUNDATION of the coven. Pray on the names of Bible characters who embody and/or demonstrate this energy. I love the Daughters of Zelophehad and what they stand for. When I form a Christian Witches Coven, if all the members are anchoring Yin energy, I'm definitely proposing this name! The formal name would be: **The Daughters of Zelophehad Christian Witches Coven of Salem** (the location can be added to the end of the name, if desired).

The members can select and propose several names, then practice divination for the most appropriate selection. Remember: the name is the nature.

Coven Colors

This may sound trivial, yet color is of extreme importance. The colors of the Christian Witches Mystery School are black (for the darkness we love as witches, the field of potentiality, the no-thing-ness), red (for blood, fiery passion and heart), and purple (for the crown chakra and all things royal, divine and ascended).

Selecting coven colors will be a group experience, so use divination. Start with the 7 colors of the rainbow, which are the chakra colors. Coven colors should have deep symbolism and meaning for all members. If desired, your coven may eventually have its own attire, such as magick robes (for ritual and ceremony) and shirts (for casual occasions) and more. These can be in the coven's colors. Altar cloths can also be procured in the coven's colors. Have fun with it!

The Reliquary

The reliquary is the chest that contains all the sacred, magickal implements of the coven. If your coven doesn't have a permanent home for coven use only, the implements will have to be transported for each meeting.

The shared magickal implements of the coven are gathered by all members, according to divination and synchronicity, and are stored in a sealed chest in between meetings. The chest can be entrusted to the person who is the Keeper of the Reliquary (a coven leadership role). Be mindful that this person will be entrusted with powerful magickal tools. They will be responsible for transporting and storing the same.

NEVER use personal magickal implements in coven rituals, and vice versa. EVERYTHING IS ENERGY.

Coven Meeting Agenda

As with all sacred occasions, the following can be included:

- Cleanse and clear the space.
- Prayer (if the prayers are not written out, select Psalms that are appropriate).
- Prepare the magickal implements.
- Altar construction.
- Calling in the spirit team.
- Candle lighting ceremony.
- Meditation.
- Intention for the ritual/ceremony/meeting.
- Divination for the ritual.
- Cast the circle and conduct the ritual (full moon ritual/new moon ritual or other sacred ritual that supports the coven).
- Completion and thanksgiving.
- Clean up.
- Eat/break bread.

Be sure to include any other inspirations you and the coven are divinely led to engage in.

As an educational value add for the members, invite those who practice other magickal systems to come and speak to your coven so that you all continue to learn and grow in your knowledge and understanding of all systems of magick. Even if you don't practice these systems, understanding them can foster a deeper sense of camaraderie in the global magickal community and will ultimately make you a better magician.

Coven Services

If all coven members are in agreement, your coven can perform spiritual services for its members, and the community at large. There are many people who don't have a church home, and would like to have rituals and/or ceremonies performed to mark rites of passage or special occasions. Since the coven may have initiated witches as members, it could offer:

- Baby blessings
- Weddings (especially Pagan weddings)
- Teen Rites of Passage
- Wedding Anniversaries
- Healing circles/Meditations/Classes and/or workshops on magick and the craft
- Any celebration that calls for a ritual that a witch can perform

Coven Grimoire

Acquire a Coven Grimoire so that all can record their name and sigil in the book, and so that all the magickal rites, rituals and protocols of the coven can be written out clearly. The Coven Grimoire can be stored in the reliquary when not in use at coven meetings. It's critically important that absolutely **NO ONE** touches or lays eyes on any of the coven's magickal implements who isn't currently a member of the coven, especially the Coven Grimoire.

3-Part Clarion Call to Christian Witches Everywhere

I will end this treatise with a 3-part clarion call to Christian Witches everywhere:

1 - EXIT THE BROOM CLOSET

There are far too many Christian Witches still hiding in broom closets due to fear.

To hide is to "put or keep out of sight; conceal from the view or notice of others." Hiding is in conflict with Christ's teaching to "Let your light so shine before men, that they may see your good works, and glorify your Father which is in heaven." (Matthew 5:16 KJV)

Let's go deeper.

In the Magickal Arts & Sciences, we have the 'inner mysteries' and the 'outer court.' The inner mysteries are only granted to deserving initiates who have proven worthy by enduring the trials of initiation. The outer court consists of the publicly known information about a magickal tradition, the publicly accessible spaces, public rituals and/or public events of the magickal order.

For instance, we may know much about Yoruba from family members, friends or others we know who are Yoruba. They haven't hidden the fact that they're Yoruba. When one is initiated as a Yoruba Priest or Priestess, they are inducted into the 'inner mysteries' to deeper and deeper degrees. It's public knowledge that they are becoming initiated, because every Yoruba Priest/Priestess I know was required to wear all white clothing for an entire year before the bembe, or celebration. If you're anywhere in the sphere of this initiate, it would be next to impossible to be unaware that this person is Yoruba.

A similar experience exists in the Akan path. An Akan Priestess shared with me that during their initiation they must eat all food exclusively with their hands for a period of one year. As with all trials of initiation, there's a specific purpose for this practice. It would be impossible, therefore, to not know that this person is becoming initiated as an Akan Priestess when they're eating every meal with their fingers. Someone is bound to ask questions at some point.

I don't know the inner mysteries of Yoruba or Akan. I'm not Yoruba. I'm not Akan. Yet I know many Yoruba and Akan Priests and Priestesses who are not hiding the fact that they Yoruba or Akan. Still, they aren't giving us the inner mysteries either.

There's a balance to strike that a Christian Witch must be ever so mindful of: keeping the inner mysteries, while sharing the outer court.

Let's examine another example. In the Hebrew Bible, construction of the tabernacle was clearly defined. There was an outer courtyard where all the Israelites were called to gather. Then there was a 'holy' compartment, where only the priests entered. Finally, there was a 'most holy' compartment where only the high priest could enter, and then only once per year on Atonement Day.

Let's look at one more example. Christ taught the masses. He performed miracles and works of sorcery publicly (more about Jesus being a sorcerer is in the amazing book **Magic of Christianity**). Thousands of people witnessed these events. Countless were healed and/or helped. Then there were the teachings, with the deeper esoteric meaning, that were reserved for the 12 apostles and the women who accompanied them, including the one whom some have said was the primary disciple and a powerful teacher in her own right: Mary Magdalene.

Again we observe the 'outer court' and the 'inner mysteries.'

No one is asking you to spill the secrets of Christian Witchcraft on Facebook. Indeed, it would be foolish, reckless and out of divine order to put the inner mysteries in front of those who are not initiated (or becoming initiated). These inner mysteries are powerful such that they would prove harmful in the hands of the spiritually immature, weak-minded, vengeful and those with a toxic emotional body.

The issue is with **hiding** the fact that you're a Christian Witch. No one hides the fact that they won a beauty pageant, or received the Pulitzer prize, or went sky diving. These are high points in our lives which we enthusiastically share with those we love (even if we don't blast it on social media).

Coming to the spiritual realization that you're a Christian Witch (monumental) and actually deciding to walk that path (magnificent) is a high point in one's soul unfoldment that deserves the highest regard, from yourself, within yourself, for yourself. YOU WON! Again, this does not mean you blast it on social media. Our social media profiles are as distinct as each one of us.

It's simply a matter of living your life authentically as a Christian Witch, speaking authentically (with no editing), dressing authentically, engaging the ceremonies and rituals you desire, and BEING AND DOING YOU. No hiding. No fear. This is a magnificent path. Why would we hide? Christ didn't hide, and was absolutely considered a maverick.

A radical act of self-love is to allow yourself to be loved through and through, for who you truly are, witch and all. If we hide such an important aspect of self, the people who love us are loving us for who they think we are, and not for who we truly are. In that scenario, we're not allowing ourselves to experience the totality of love. Yes, it's scary to let oneself be seen through and through. This is the true meaning of intimacy: 'into me see.'

I promise you, beyond the scariness of being seen for who you truly are, is the rapturous experience of being loved unconditionally through and through, witch and all. Everyone in my life, and especially those in my intimate space, knows, loves and appreciates me as a witch, otherwise, they're not around. As you know from my sharing with you here, the process wasn't instant and it wasn't pretty. It was, however, vital to my unfoldment.

2 - SPEAK UP

Witches are still being persecuted in 2020. The witch camps of Ghana are just one example. We have work to do on this planet Christian Witches.
   That work is the work of spiritual liberation.
   FREEDOM OF WORSHIP and FREEDOM OF DEVOTION are birthrights of ALL.
   That's the job of people like us... people who understand marginalization, judgment, persecution and being outcasts. We understand these experiences because witches have endured these, and far worse, for thousands of years. Magickal people can be misunderstood. People with powers are often considered dangerous. This must stop.
   Your voice is vital to the global transformation unfolding as we enter the Age of Aquarius.
   We need you to speak up. Not everyone speaks up in the same way. Do it in your own way. We're counting on you. Whole generations of people have suffered and died because no one was willing to speak up. Where ever you do it, and however you're led to do it, it's time to SPEAK UP.

3 - SHARE YOUR GIFTS

This is a simple one. It's what we all long to do on a visceral, soul level... serve and share who we truly are. It's why we're here. The real travesty in being in the broom closet is that the gifts deposited in you from Source go unused. The graveyard is full of potential.
   Service to humanity as Christian Witches is especially important now, when the world is changing at an alarmingly fast rate, and it's becoming easier to lose deep connection with nature because we're so entranced by technology.
   Sharing your gifts has become essential. At this point, one could even argue it's critical.

I'll say it again: **WE NEED YOU NOW WITCHES**.

Let's do this.

I love you.

About the Author

Rev. Valerie Love (aka KAISI) is a practicing Christian Witch, author of 18 books on spirituality, metaphysics, Christian Witchcraft and the occult, and speaks globally to audiences who are seeking this information.

She is the founding teacher of the Covenant of Christian Witches Mystery School in the Solomonic Tradition (CCW for short) and the creator of the Christian Witches Facebook Page where thousands of Christian Witches love on each other and where KAISI regularly does 'Witchy Wednesday' videos. You'll also find the occasional witchy meme, because we just can't help it.

KAISI leads retreats globally, including Ayahausa ceremonies in the Andes mountains of Peru, where you're invited to, as Kush, a shaman we love, says "drink more plants."

Though her collection of witch hats has grown completely out of control, that fact doesn't stop KAISI from procuring more.

Christian Witches has a Patreon community where you can contribute any amount monthly to the creation of the Mystery School and books on Christian Witchcraft.

The Christian Witches YouTube channel features content on Bible Magick, sorcery, Tarot and all things Christian Witchcraft.

You are invited to deeply engage — and become active in — the Christian Witches movement.

You are loved!

You can connect with me on:
- https://www.christianwitches.com
- https://www.facebook.com/ChristianWitches
- https://www.instagram.com/christianwitches
- https://www.patreon.com/ChristianWitches
- https://www.youtube.com/c/christianwitches

Also by Valerie Love

Blessings beautiful soul! THANK YOU for buying and reading this book! If you've found this book valuable, you may also enjoy the following related works for your path as a Christian Witch. Would you also kindly leave a review on Amazon? Reviews help tremendously!

CONFESSIONS OF A CHRISTIAN WITCH: HOW AN EX-JEHOVAH'S LIVES MAGICKAL & HOW YOU CAN TOO!
Because confession is good for the soul, if not for the reputation, I do hereby confess that I...Had no idea what a Christian Witch was, never heard the term, and would never have chosen to be one, had it not been for a burst of inspiration that literally spoke it through my mouth on October 22, 2011, the day I came out of the proverbial broom closet publicly as a Christian Witch...

CHRISTIAN WITCHES MANIFESTO: A CHRISTIAN WITCHES MANIFESTO & HOW TO WRITE YOUR OWN
This 10-Tenet Manifesto for Christian Witches is for you if you're anything like me... I had ideas in my mind of what I knew to be true as a Christian Witch, and what I hold dear to me on my path. I knew it had to be in writing. Here is the result.

Made in the USA
Coppell, TX
06 June 2021